KIPLING'S VISION

KIPLING'S VISION

A Study in his Short Stories

Sukeshi Kamra

PRESTIGE

PRESTIGE BOOKS
New Delhi

Published by
PRESTIGE BOOKS
3/28, East Patel Nagar, New Delhi 110 008
in association with
Indian Society for Commonwealth Studies
New Delhi.

Rs. 400
Prestige Books
International

1989

ISBN 81-85218-04-8

Phototypesetting by
data culture
C 15, Amar Colony, Lajpat Nagar IV
New Delhi 110 065

Printed by
Efficient Offset Printers, Delhi.

Contents

Preface

Rudyard Kipling has often been dismissed as a man of insignificant literary merit, and his critics find it hard to account for the Nobel Prize that he won in 1907. Though attempts have been made to "resurrect" him, they are, more often than not, based on his most popular works such as *The Jungle Books*, *Kim*, and his later short stories.

The aim of this book is to consider and analyse the vision of one of the very few literary men who have managed to combine journalism, literature, and the wisdom of the seer in such a way as to produce a sensitive analysis of the modern age, alienation and fragmentation have become cliched words today, but, at the *fin-de-siécle*, they were just being introduced into the literary register. Catastrophes assumed social rather than individual proportions, and Kipling, in analysing and presenting the moral and spiritual abyss within man was attempting to do something rather new with fiction. Tales which deal with these aspects of chaos have been chosen for detailed analysis. Most of them are early short stories, some of which were written for newspapers, and put together in three collections under the titles *Plain Tales From the Hills*, *The Phantom Rickshaw and Other Tales*, and *Life's Handicap, Being Stories of Mine Own People*.

A damsel with a dulcimer
In a vision once I saw:
It was an abyssinian maid,
And on her dulcimer she played,
Singing of Mount Abora.
Could I revive within me
Her symphony and song,
To such a deep delight 'would win me

That with music loud and long,
I would build that dome in air,
That sunny dome ! those caves of ice !
And all who heard should see them there,
And all should cry, Beware ! Beware !
His flashing eyes, his floating hair !
Weave a circle round him thrice,
And close your eyes with holy dread.,
For he on honey-dew hath fed,
And drunk the milk of Paradise.

S. T. Coleridge, "Kubla Khan"

Introduction

I

The most striking feature of Kipling's vision is its uncanny affinity with that of the poets of the Romantic Period, who recorded the first major crisis after the period of enlightenment in the fifteenth and sixteenth centuries,[1] and with the vision of a number of twentieth century writers and dramatists such as Camus, Kafka, Beckett and Weiss. Thus, in his role as "seer" and "prophet," as Eliot referred to him,[2] Kipling includes time--past, present and future--when addressing himself to the problems of the human condition.

M.H. Abrams, in *Natural Supernaturalism*, while discussing the concern of the Romantics to find a way to "redeem" man, states that this concern was an "element in a set of interrelated concepts which had wide currency in the age of Wordsworth and Coleridge," concepts which have "evolved into the reigning diagnosis of our own age of anxiety: the claim that man, who was once well is now ill, and that at the core of the modern malaise lies his fragmentation, dissociation, estrangement or alienation. The individual has becomne radically split in three main aspects. He is divided within himself, he is divided from other men, and he is divided from his environment."[3] This, as I see it, is Kipling's major concern in the short stories of the three collections under discussion, namely, *Plain Tales From the Hills*, *Phantom Rickshaw and Other Tales*, and *Life's Handicap, Being Stories of Mine Own People*.[4] Whereas some tales, in all collections, deal with trivial but interesting details of British India, a number of them take up the problem of chaos in its various forms of alienation, psychological disintegration and agnosticism. If the Romantics were attempting to deal with the after-effects of the displacement of a mythological universe, Kipling seems to be attempting to solve the problems created by the rise of a predominantly secular world which exalted empiricism and displaced all forms that defied scientific analysis, such as the Imagination, Myth and Religion.

Kipling was not alone in his attempt to invest life with the mystery that is creation. Robert Louis Stevenson, Rider Haggard and Edgar Allan Poe, forced back the boundaries of empiricism to include all sorts of surrealistic phantoms within the self and in the macrocosm. Instead of believing that man can be fully explained in terms of social reality, they chose to believe that divinity and demonic powers exist simultaneously in man, and their tales explore these liminal areas of man's being. Thus, in Kipling's stories, the supernatural--one manifestation of the unempirical--often intrudes as that which is incomprehensible to empirical man. Yet, ironically enough, man cannot remove himself from the inexplicable. It surrounds him in the form of death, paranoia and neurosis, phenomena which destroy man's every attempt to rationalize, or create what he considers to be a well-defined, meaningful universe. In Kipling's world, for instance, Cholera symbolizes this inability to defeat the unknown powers, who themselves defy analysis.

The narrator of the tales is gifted with more understanding than the people whose experiences he narrates. While they are caught in the chaos, unable to order their existence, the narrator reveals an ability to analyse the reasons for the chaos, and is able, at times, to suggest the possible existence of order, not perceptible to the average man. In fact, in *Life's Handicap*, he achieves the status of a seer. In *Plain Tales From the Hills*, the narrator leads his reader/audience through the subliminal areas of man's unconscious, peopled by demons, ghosts, destructive fury, but also characterized by love, faith and charity, even if the last three seem to be absent at times. Alienation and fragmentation of personality make it impossible for the protagonists to live, as the others do, primarily because they cannot cultivate the "Habits" necessary for survival.[5] Therefore, death not only comes early, but is violent and frightening as well, defeating their hope that in death they will find peace. Tales which indicate the nature of Kipling's vision merit detailed analysis. Among such stories are "Thrown Away," "False Dawn," "The Gate of the Hundred Sorrows," "Beyond the Pale," "The Bisara of Pooree," "By Word of Mouth," and "To be Filed for Reference."

In the next selection under discussion, *Phantom Rickshaw and Other Tales*, Kipling states that his so-called "ghost-stories" are not mere fantastic tales, but a "collection of facts that never quite explained themselves."[6] One of the major "facts" which afflicts the protagonists is the awareness of being hounded. If the characters in *Plain Tales* suffer from the awareness of an alienation which they cannot overcome, the characters in *Phantom Rickshaw* are forced to realize that their alienation is merely a facet of the truth--that they are trapped in an exchange with ubiquitous, evil powers, which even death will not terminate. The empirical world thus broadens to include the surrealistic world within the self, a world which releases the phantom of Mrs Keith-Wessington to torture Jack Pansay in "Phantom Rickshaw"; makes Morrowbie Jukes believe that he has lived in the land of the living-dead for a lifetime in "The Strange Ride of Morrowbie Jukes," and drives Peachey Carnehan in "The Man Who Would Be King," to a sort of divine madness. Agony characterizes their condition, and the terror that comes of the encounter with forces beyond definition.

It is in *Life's Handicap*, that the narrator records his own encounters with the powers of darkness. Tales such as "Bubbling Well Road," and "The Mark of the Beast," reveal his confrontation with the horrifying, powerful forces that somehow seem an externalization of the subconscious in man. In tales such as "The City of Dreadful Night," the whole of mankind is seen labouring under the fetters of this inescapable evil, epitomized in the deathly pall created by the omnipresent killer disease, cholera. The narrator, however, seems to emerge from the darkness and despair of night to the glory and promise of the day. Mankind, of whom and to whom he speaks, does not perceive the order which dictates death and life, and thus suffers, unrelieved by the power of the imagination. Death destroys the socially precarious relationship between Holden and Ameera suddenly but irrevocably in "Without Benefit of Clergy"; as suddenly, it destroys thousands of pilgrims at the feet of their gold in the same tale. It makes the "Wandering Jew" lead a death-in-life existence in his desperate attempt to escape the horror it signifies in the tale of the same name, while the dark powers come and claim Hummeil, a young but tortured man in "At the End of the Passage."

The tales are, however, framed by the Preface (at the beginning), and "L'envoi" (at the end of the selection). They seem to suggest the contrary of death and despair, for both these aspects of darkness are assimilated into a larger whole, the "Great Overseer" of "L'envoi." The narrator appears to realize the dualistic nature of reality and Kipling, the story-teller and narrator, prophesies the existence of order where chaos seems to reign supreme. Kipling's quest echoes that of the

Romantics in their search for wholeness. The seer believes that the divine order can be created on earth by finding, in the words of Abrams, "the way to a reintegration which will restore" man's "unity with himself, his community with his fellowmen and his companionability with an alien and hostile outer world."[7] The way to such a reintegration forms part of Kipling's vision. It can be achieved through exploiting the qualities which make man divine, in "God's image."[8] Some of these qualities are Love, Imagination, and the Law which dictates self-fulfilment.

My main concern in this book is, however, to analyse tales which offer an insight into Kipling's profound understanding of what is commonly referred to today as the dark side of man's soul, the shadowy, unexplored regions which made Conrad's Mr. Kurtz, a character created in about the same period, exclaim on his death-bed: "The horror ! The horror !"[9] Before analysing the tales, I would like to outline the nature of the critical response to the short stories and in particular, to the nature of Kipling's vision, from his own time to the present day.

II

In 1888, *Plain Tales From the Hills* was published in England, and the literary world was forced into noticing the precocity of Kipling, one of the "lesser breed" of journalists, who seemed to invest the subject of his tales, India, with a charm which made Andrew Lang exclaim in 1889: "It may safely be said that *Plain Tales From the Hills* will reach more of India, of our task there, of the various peoples whom we try to rule, than many Blue books."[10] However, most of his contemporaries regarded Kipling as an insignificant literary man but a good journalist, who excelled in the knowledge of his subject but lacked a literary style.

It was with the publication of *Life's Handicap*, that Kipling gained popularity in literary circles, and most critics agreed that the selection contained some of his best stories. Supporters used it as triumphant proof of his literary merit. Edmund Gosse, writing in 1891, believed that "if the remainder of his writings were swept away, posterity would be able to reconstruct its Rudyard Kipling from 'Without Benefit of Clergy,' 'The Man Who Would Be King,' 'The Strange Ride of Morrowbie Jukes,' and 'Beyond the Pale.' " More than that, if all record of Indian habits had been destroyed, much might be conjectured from them of the pathos, the splendour, the cruelty and the mystery of India."[11] *The Bookman* gave *Life's Handicap* a very favourable review, asserting that "he who leisurely turns the pages will seek and find more than amusement," and outlined Kipling's major themes: "Men, and in a lesser degree women and children--even brutes, as dogs, apes and elephants, in so far as they present inchoate human elements--are Mr.Kipling's absorbing theme."[12] Even Henry James, in a famous letter to William James in 1892, conceded: "Kipling strikes me personally as the most complete man of genius (as distinct from fine intelligence) that I have ever known."[13]

The first major attack on Kipling for "brutality, warmongering and illiberalism," came in 1899 in an article titled "The Voice of the Hooligan," by Robert Buchanan. He picked on Kipling's journalistic beginnings and centred his whole argument on his being in "vogue" with the "spirit of the times," of "ephemeral journalism,"[14] which, in his opinion, exalted "all that is ignorant, selfish, base, and brutal in the instincts of humanity" (p. 240). In fact, Kipling was often accused of not having any "sympathy with humanity."[15] Sir Walter Besant replied to this open challenge to all Kipling admirers in an article titled: "Is it the Voice of the Hooligan ?" in 1900. For the first time, Kipling's mastery over the short story form was acclaimed. Thus, Besant states, "Another reason why we who are not critics delight in Kipling is that he gives us short stories."[16]

In the early decades of the twentieth century, Kipling came in for tremendous censure for what was considered to be his "Imperialistic" political stance, which was, needless to say, rigorously applied to all his work. In 1919, T.S. Eliot made an attempt to rescue Kipling from obscurity and referred to him as a "neglected celebrity." He acclaimed *Plain Tales* as "the one perfect picture of a society of English, narrow, snobbish, spiteful, ignorant and vulgar, set down absurdly in a continent of which they are unconscious."[17] Bonamy Dobrée in 1927, in an article titled "Rudyard Kipling," joined forces with Eliot to prove that "Mr. Kipling has so scrupulously winnowed the elements of his art, that his candour has deceived many into thinking him too near a simpleton to yield much that can be of use to them in exploring life."[18] It is in an anonymous article, published a week after his death in 1836, that the attempt to fuse Kipling's mastery over the short story form and his subject matter (which made such a form so eminently suitable) was made: "Rudyard Kipling is first of all master of the conte ... The short story was suited to his peculiar gifts of compassion, of clarity, of characterization. ... He has employed the grotesque, the horrible, and very often eerie in his plots, looking with anxious but never credulous eyes at what may be distinguished or imagined 'at the end of the passage' in the half-world betwixt fact and dream."[19]

However, Kipling criticism received its first major impetus in 1941, when two famous articles, one not very favourable, were published. One was an article by Edmund Wilson, "The Kipling That Nobody Read," and the other an introduction to Kipling's verse by T.S. Eliot. The latter seems to have felt it incumbent on him to defend Kipling against his critics, as he admitted in an address to the Kipling Society in 1958. During the course of this address, he isolated two aspects of Kipling which seemed to him to be of special importance, those of the "moralist," and the "seer."[20] It is Kipling the seer that Dobrée celebrates in *Rudyard Kipling: Realist and Fabulist*, published in 1967. He quotes Maurois as saying that "Kipling had a permanent and natural contact with the oldest and deepest layers of human consciousness,"[21] part of which requires an awareness of the "individuality which in each case has to contend with an abysmal sense of individual nothingness," and "the horror of great darkness" (pp. 29-30), as well as the power to see "an extraordinary, even extravagant delight ... in life, in the doings of mankind" (p. 33). Therefore, for the first time, Eliot's judgement of Kipling as a seer received the analysis it merits. Even though Kipling seems to have found a good reception after his death, critics like Yeats and later, Lionel Trilling, dismissed him as lacking the qualities which make a great artist. As had become commonplace in Kipling criticism, Trilling in *The Liberal Imagination* (1949), criticised Kipling for being sympathetic with the "administrator" and for his so-called "hatred of the liberal intellect."[22] All in all, Trilling believes that Kipling did untold "harm to the national virtues" (p. 96).

Criticism of Kipling in the last three decades has matured enough to leave opinions on his political stance out of the critical evaluation of his merit as an artist. Noel Annan, in "Kipling's Place in the History of Ideas" tries to analyse the thematic concerns of the short stories. According to him,"the centre of Kipling's world is society itself,"[23] and the "impression which his work as a whole gives is that of a man who sees human beings moving in a definable network of social relationships which impose upon them a code of behaviour appropriate to their environment" (p. 102). This, Annan believes, is clearly demonstrated in Kipling's tales on India, where, Indian society "politically, nervously, physically, and spiritually quivered on the edge of a precipice" (p. 102). The forces which prevent the structure from going over the precipice are, according to Annan's analysis of Kipling's stance, "religion, law, custom, convention, morality--the forces of social control--which impose upon individuals certain rules which they broke at their peril" (p. 104). Consequently, Annan criticizes Kipling for what he considers to be his inability to show "the effect . . . of the social process on the individual" (p. 124).

Annan at least conceded that Kipling took a modern approach to the problem of individual and society. Gilbert, in *The Good Kipling* (1970), carries this argument a little further to prove that tales such as "Without Benefit of Clergy" are in many ways "surprisingly modern--almost, indeed, existential,"[24] and he goes on to compare that story with Hemingway's *A Farewell to Arms*. According to Gilbert, there are a few essential truths in Kipling's world: "first, that man is alone in a blank cosmos where he is ruled by impersonal law; second, that through a highly conscious act of commitment to the reality of his own experience he can rescue himself from life's irrationality; and finally, that by doing this, he secures for himself a meaningful freedom, albeit within the larger framework of the absurd" (pp. 209-10). Shamsul Islam too believes that there are redemptive features in Kipling's vision, contained within his concept of the "Law." According to him, "Kipling's law is composed of three main inter-related elements, namely, moral values, the Imperial Idea and the Doctrine of Action. It is with this code of life that Kipling opposes the Dark Powers which he encounters everywhere."[25]

Most critics, then, seem to agree that Kipling's tales reveal the dark side of existence as well as the forces of good. However, most of those involved in explicating the "Law" in his works forego a detailed analysis of the early tales, which merit such analysis primarily because they reveal his profound understanding of, and sympathy for, the tormented individuals born into a disintegrating social fabric. In his very first published work, *Plain Tales From the Hills*, Kipling introduced the public to such tortured beings, who represent the modern experience of alienation.

NOTES

1.M.H.Abrams, *Natural Supernaturalism* (New York: Norton and Co., 1971), p. 145. All further references to the book are to this edition.

2. T.S.Eliot, in an address given to the Kipling society in 1958. The complete address is included by Elliot L.Gilbert in *Kipling and the Critics* (New York: New York U. Press, 1965), p. 121. All further references to Gilbert's book are to this edition.

3. M.H.Abrams, *Natural Supernaturalism*, p. 145.

4. *Plain Tales From the Hills* was first published in 1888; *The Phantom Rickshaw and Other Tales* in 1888 as well; and *Life's Handicap, Being Stories of Mine Own People* in 1891. All bibliographical information on Kipling's works is from *Rudyard Kipling: A Bibliographical Catalogue* by James McG.Stewart, ed. A.W.Yeats (Toronto: Dalhousie U. Press, 1959).

5. Samuel Beckett in an essay on Proust, quoted in full by Martin Esslin in his chapter on Beckett in *The Theatre of the Absurd* (Garden City: Anchor, 1969). This term, and my use of it in analysing *Plain Tales* is discussed more fully in Chapter I.

6. Rudyard Kipling, *The Phantom Rickshaw and Other Tales* (New York: A.L.Burt, 1900), Preface.

7. M.H.Abrams, *Natural Supernaturalism*, p. 145.

8. William Blake's poem "The Divine Image" is extremely relevant here, and I quote the first three stanzas:

> To Mercy Pity Peace and Love,
> All pray in their distress:
> And to these virtues of delight
> Return their thankfulness.

For Mercy Pity Peace and Love
Is God our father dear:
And Mercy Pity Peace and Love
Is man his child and care.

For Mercy has a human heart
Pity, a human face:
And Love, the human form divine,
And Peace the human dress.

The poem is taken from *Blake's Poetry and Designs*, ed. Mary L. Johnson and John E. Grant (London: W. W. Norton, 1979), p. 30.

9. Joseph Conrad, *Heart of Darkness* (New York: Doubleday and Co., 1969), p. 118.

10. Andrew Lang, in a review for the *Daily News* (1889), collected in *Kipling: The Critical Heritage*, ed. R.L.Green (New York: Barnes and Noble, 1971), p. 48. All references to the book (C.H.) are to this edition.

11. Edmund Gosse, in a review in the *Century Magazine*, 1891, collected in *C.H.*, p. 117.

12. *The Bookman*, anonymous review in 1891. Collected in *C.H.*, pp. 129-30.

13. Henry James, in a letter dated 6 Feb., 1892. Collected in *C.H.*, p. 69.

14. Robert Buchanan, in the *Contemporary Review*, 1899. Collected in *C.H.*, p. 242.

15. J.M.Barrie, in a review in the *Contemporary Review*, 1891. Collected in *C.H.*, p. 85.

16. Sir Walter Besant, in a review in the *Contemporary Review*, 1900. Collected in C.H., p. 253.

17. T.S.Eliot, in a review in the *Athenaeum*, 1919. Collected in *C.H.*, p. 322.

18. Bonamy Dobrée, "Rudyard Kipling," *Monthly Criterion*, Dec. 1927. Collected in *C.H.*, p. 342.

19. Anonymous review in the *Times Literary Supplement*, 25 Jan., 1936. Collected in *C.H.*, p. 386.

20. T. S. Eliot, "The Unfading Genius of Rudyard Kipling," *Kipling and the Critics*, ed. Gilbert, p. 121.

21. Bonamy Dobrée, *Rudyard Kipling: Realist and Fabulist* (London: Oxford U. Press, 1967), p. 29. All references to the book are to this edition.

22. Lionel Trilling, "Kipling," *Kipling and the Critics*, ed. Gilbert, p. 96. All references to the articles are to this reprint.

23. Noel Annan, "Kipling's Place in the History of Ideas," *Kipling's Mind and Art*, ed. Andrew Rutherford (London: Oliver and Boyd, 1965), p. 99. All further references to Annan's article are to its reprint in this collection.

24. Elliot L. Gilbert, *The Good Kipling* (Oberlin: Ohio U. Press, 1970), p. 41. All further references are to this edition.

25. Shamsul Islam, *Kipling's "Law": A Study of his Philosophy of Life* (London: Macmillan, 1975), p. 144.

Plain Tales From the Hills

I

A veil 'twixt us and Thee, dread Lord
A veil 'twixt us and Thee:
Lest we should hear too clear, too clear
And unto madness see ![1]

Such is the prayer of the sensitive mortal who inhabits Kipling's fictional world in *Plain Tales From the Hills*. The "veil," as Miriam Cohen intuitively perceives, is necessary if man is to retain his sanity, as the truth which it hides is incomprehensible to man, and thus frightening as well. But for some, the veil is rent and the confrontation with the dreaded truth that lies beyond spells disaster. It leads "The Boy" in the tale "Thrown Away"[2] to commit suicide; the lover in "False Dawn"[3] to propose marriage to the wrong lady; the opium addicts in "The Gate of the Hundred Sorrows"[4] to lead a death-in-life existence, which is even then torturous. The list is never ending. Kipling's tales spin out the tragic experience that these characters undergo because they see "too clear" one of the inescapable problems facing modern man[5]--that of alienation. The attempt to deal with this problem leads these characters not only to physical disintegration, in the form of death, but a fragmentation of the spirit which animates the physical being.

It is natural therefore, for Kipling the young visionary struggling to come to terms with the brutal truth of man's condition, to anchor his analysis of the problem of alienation by considering a community alienated from its natural surroundings, namely, the British in India.[7] Alienated from a country which symbolised order, harmony and empiricism, the British in India, as Kipling sees them, are totally incapable of dealing with a country which seems to thrive on the reverse of this very order. For them, India is a mind-boggling manifestation of the principle of chaos. The dramatic changes of climate, the meteoric temperament of the native, the spiritual inclusiveness that incorporates the "Powers of Darkness" as well as the divine forces which link man with the cosmos, elude the understanding of the British empiricist. Thus, the famed "Oriental passion" is incomprehensible to Trejago, the protagonist in "Beyond the Pale," who continues to look at "things from a Western standpoint,"[8] though he is no longer in the West. The mysterious emanations of the Bisara of Pooree, in the tale of the same name, is merely an "interesting bit of folklore" to Churton, the average Colonial. The very physical temperament of the Indian landscape is indefinable to the Britisher and hence assumes frightening proportions. Against India, "men stand out all crude and raw, with nothing to tone them down and nothing to scale them against." (p. 310)

In order to deal with the terrifying awareness of alienation, man , in Kipling's fictional world, cultivates the "habit"[9] mentioned by Beckett, to protect him from being forced to face the fact of alienation. Thus, "they," that is the British in India "do their work, grow to think that there is nothing but their work, and nothing like their work," as the narrator comments in "Wressley of the Foreign Office."[10] The attempt to form a little England in India, is one of the several means used to battle against the terrifying reality of alienation that the British feel in India. Generally, therefore, the only feature common to the native and British sections of any Indian city is the "overarching sky."[11] The prayer of the exiled in India is, understandably, "to escape where amusement is amusement and a reputation worth having" (p. 17).

Against a community set in an essentially alien atmosphere, Kipling places people--mainly British in this selection--who are unable to create the necessary "veil" or conform to the general "habits" created by society. As a result, they "see too clear," and the sight destroys them, or leaves them burdened with a death wish. For them, "the suffering of being"[12] is not relieved by the kind of "habit' which makes such moments of realization bearable to man.

It is about these people, that some of Kipling's best tales in *Plain Tales From the Hills* are written. In the tragic experience of these individuals is contained Kipling's starkly honest analysis of the truths of modern existence. It is important, before considering the vision itself, to remember that the vision is presented through the medium of a narrator. The characters and their experiences form part of his repertoire of tales, as the narrator himself forms part of Kipling's imagination. Thus, Kipling's vision in *Plain Tales* is a complex whole which includes the experience of the characters and the narrator's interpretation of it. The narrator, in this selection, reveals the tragedy that defines the existence of some of the characters, and analyses the cause of the tragedy, but is unable to offer a solution to their problems.

II

> Some--there are losses in every trade--
> Will break their hearts 'ere bitted and made,
> Will fight like fiends as the rope cuts hard
> And die dumb mad in the breaking yard.
>
> (Epigram to "Thrown Away")

These alienated souls, should, according to the narrator, be sent "home" as soon as possible, to prevent them from "sinking" (p. 327) altogether. While in "ninety-nine cases out of a hundred," the "heat and the knowledge of having lost money and health" is enough to "sober the newcomer" to India, the hundredth case is that of the exception, those who "break their hearts 'ere bitted and made" (p. 15). Among these is The Boy in "Thrown Away," who commits suicide because, in the words of the narrator, he is "too sensitive and took things seriously" (p. 19). What is an "ordinary Colonel's wigging" to the others is an unbearable disgrace to him. Not only is he removed from "home," but alienated from the rest of his fellow countrymen in India. Saumarez, the protagonist in "False Dawn," unlike the average Britisher, holds the "balance hair true" between the two Misses Copleigh. The difficulty he experiences in upsetting this balance by professing (in the manner society demands) to love one to the exclusion of the other, is apparently not felt by this society. The narrator speaks for society when he states that Saumarez "made up his mind . . . to marry the elder one, or at least we all made sure he would," which according to the narrator, "comes to the same thing" (p. 43). There exists, therefore, a basic dislocation between him and society. Similarly, in "Beyond the Pale," Trejago is alienated from the society around him because of a difference in outlook. He attempts to solve the problem of alienation, not by cultivating the habit of frequenting the "Club," but by wandering into the forbidden native sections of the city. However, his isolation is so strong that even the attempt to overcome it by creating a bond between himself and Bisesa is doomed to failure.

"The Gate of the Hundred Sorrows" opens to reveal a group of lonely individuals, for whom oblivion is bliss and anything that provides this oblivion, divine. Even then, the agony is never quite overcome and Misquitta's monologue is punctuated with the revealing phrase: "I don't care." Like The Boy and Trejago, Misquitta has no sustaining emotional bonds. He has surrendered the only bond he had created, through marriage, to the "black smoke," as he terms opium. The physical world is, for him, "the clean cool mat" on which he rests his drug-debased body. Communication with the world beyond the Gate is similarly reduced to a monologue through the filtering medium of opium. The hallucinatory vision of "red and black dragons" engaged in a continuous fight is more real to him than is the world of men.

The sense of total isolation which pursues these characters further results in a solipsistic concern with their own misery; being removed from the rest of the world, they see only their own misery. The obsessiveness which this implies is revealed by McIntosh Jelalludin in the crude but agonised fragments of poetry which he writes. His "fall" from the "light of the sun / and alone" (p. 325), haunts him as it does the others, but "the stone" as each of the other stones, "knows only her life is accursed / As she sinks in the depths of the Tarn / And alone" (p. 326). This solipsistic despair is the price these characters pay for seeing "too clear" into the void.

III

The attempt to deal with bewildering problem of alienation, therefore, leads these sensitive characters to physical, emotional and spiritual fragmentation, so that most of them welcome death as the end of an extremely painful process of suffering. The Boy courts death when his attempts at establishing a meaningful relationship with the collective "we"--of which the narrator forms a part--are frustrated. As the narrator crudely states, "he had gone away to die like a poisoned rat"

(p. 22). He has been poisoned by society, which rejects non-conformists, and clearly he is regarded as being one. He consistently refuses to "stand steady," and is therefore a threat to the community which requires him to do so. Instead, frustration leads him to indulge in frenzied activity which costs him not only his health and money, but also his life, as the collective "we" will not tolerate his "heartbreaking" search for the security his parents offered him "all his days, from the hour he was born till the hour he went into Sandhurst" (p. 16). To them, he is a high spirited animal, a "capricious puppy," an unbridled horse, or an "overhandled colt" (p. 18).[13] But, because The Boy himself takes another view altogether of the "average" man's opinion of him, death becomes a release from the "disgrace he was unable to bear" (p. 22). For an individual like him, who sees "too clear" the "folly" and "waste" of life, suicide is the inevitable end. It is the culminating point of a process which began with his emergence into the Blakian world of harsh experience. Each new experience--from Sandhurst to living in a third-rate depot battalion to India--leaves him a little less "high" (p. 16), a little less optimistic, and a little more fragmented, and this process results in untimely death.

The world which lies behind "The Gate of the Hundred Sorrows," epitomizes just such a disintegration of the self into death. In fact, the two outstanding objects in this "chandoo-khana" are a concretization of the atmosphere of death. A "lacquered black coffin" has pride of place in the "upper room" where the customers smoke the "black smoke." Besides the coffin, "the Joss," all "green and blue and purple with age" (p. 279) acts as a constant reminder of the process of decay and putrefaction. Misquitta forms part of this slow erosion of sensibility which makes him share a sense of comradeship with the Joss. Over the years, he has degenerated into the non-human, as his mind, and by inference his imagination, surrenders to the destructive power of opium. The mind, no longer concerns itself with the essentials of man's existence, such as the major concept of Time, for "time doesn't matter" (p. 281) in a world of deadened sensibility. If the past is an amorphous reality "hundred and hundreds of years old" (p. 281), the present is a timeless moment of opium induced contentment, which leaves Misquitta not "drunk happy, you know," as he states, but "always quiet and soothed and contented" (p. 282).

However, Misquitta is aware that the contentment is an illusion sustained by opium, and as his mind disintegrates beneath the influence of the drug, it becomes steadily more difficult for him to escape into the world of divine contentment.[14] If earlier, "at the end of one's third pipe, the dragons used to move about and fight" (p. 282), it now takes "a dozen pipes to make 'em stir" (p. 282). Since opium fails to provide a permanent means of escape, Misquitta begins to yearn for death, and, paradoxically, it is for death that he lives, all else having been "over and done with long ago" (p. 281). Death is therefore synonymous with heaven which he attempted to gain "for a pice"[15] through opium and failed. It is ironical that Misquitta's addiction is a result of his desire to gain heaven on earth, because the heaven that is opium induced only helps further remove him from the world of men, an alienation which in turn agonizes him deeply. Thus, the "gate" is the perfect symbol of the isolation which leads to death as it separates the "chandoo-khana" from the real world which lies at its doorstep. Once beyond the threshold, Misquitta, as the others, leaves the Gate only in death.

The choice that these people have is between playing "Robinson Crusoe,"[16] which leads to isolation and untimely death, and living a life regulated by habit, which they are unable to do. For Dumoise, the protagonist of "By Word of Mouth,"[17] the problem of alienation is so unsurmountable that even the death of his wife is more acceptable to him, than the attempt to communicate her illness to the outside world which has neatly catalogued him as a "dormouse," and has dismissed him as inconsequential. It takes him eight days to summon enough courage to report his wife's illness to their neighbour. The delay is fatal to his wife, who dies of cholera. Though the narrator glosses over the remorse and guilt which torments Dumoise, it becomes apparent in his studious avoidance of society. Death deprives him of the only meaningful relationship in his life, and his wife's ghostly appearance seems to be mysteriously linked with a death-wish on his part. Thus, though Ram Das the native servant, is terrified at the sight of the ghost of his former mistress, Dumoise accepts the message of doom which it implies, without betraying fear or wonder at the demonic implications. All that he states is, "I shall not be sorry" (p. 323), although he recognizes that it will be an untimely end, for he still has "things to do" (p. 323). He surrenders himself without a struggle to the "Powers of Darkness."[18]

If death is not what Trejago experiences as a result of his attempt to establish a bond between Bisesa--a native woman--and himself, he is emotionally maimed for life, a mutilation which is symbolized in the "slight stiffness" in his right leg. His struggle to maintain both the life of a Britisher in India, and that of a lover, destroys them both. Bisesa undergoes physical mutilation as well, and is "walled" into a living hell, whereas Trejago is walled in by the secret which torments him, making him live the life of Eliot's hollow men. He ceases to exist, except bodily. As with The Boy and Dumoise, his spirit is broken.

These characters, while they peer into the abyss of nothingness, do not question or analyse their experience in terms of its significance. McIntosh Jelalludin, the protagonist of "To be Filed for Reference," on the other hand, comes closest to analysing intellectually the experience which has left him a shattered man. He sinks into death only after having struggled for "seven years in damnation."[19] The dark hell which was his for these seven years is not revealed to the reader. What is revealed however is a fragment of his reaction to his confrontation with the forces of darkness. The book that he leaves for posterity is an endeavour on his part to reveal the truth of his own experience--"how he lived and what befell him"--as well as that of "others" (p. 333). In writing about his experiences, Jelalludin reveals a desire to share his tragedy with others. Significantly, he dies only after he has found someone, in this case the narrator, to whom he can entrust his "monument more enduring than brass" (p. 334). Death becomes for him a means of uniting his fragmented self--body and soul, perforce separated on earth, for while his "soul" moves among the "gods," according to him, his "bestial body" writhes "down here in the garbage" (p. 331). If death is a release from the torture of earthly existence for him, for society his death is the timely end of a threat to its existence. His "monument" which testifies to the horror in life (which society has avoided facing), threatens its sense of security. So it is necessary for Strickland and the narrator to dismiss the monument of truth as a fiction created by an "extreme liar." The narrator, further, is hesitant to publish the "thing," as he terms the book, and is fearful that "the *Giant's Robe* may come true" (p. 336) in his case.

Though solipsism and alienation define the condition of these individuals till death claims them, they do make an attempt to communicate their misery to the world, if only to lessen their burden of isolation. The Boy, in his death, establishes the communication which he searched for desperately when alive, through the letter he leaves behind, fragments of which reach the reader. Misquitta, his brain eroded by years of addiction, abandons the silence of self-despair to communicate his pain to someone from the world beyond the Gate. In narrating his tale, he establishes contact with another human being, and dies soon after. Finally, McIntosh Jelalludin leaves behind his tragic experiences in the form of a work of the imagination titled "The Giant's Robe."

In the attempt of these characters to share their anguish, the narrator perceives an echo of his own desire to share his tales with his audience. However, as the characters have not found any solution to their problem, the narrator has no solution to offer either. The only truth of which he seems to be certain, is something he has learnt from "listening" to others narrating their experiences. It is a conviction that the process of story telling must be carried on. As the characters tell him their tales, he must reveal his understanding of these experiences to his audience, who may do likewise. It is in "The Rout of the White Hussars," that the narrator betrays this desire to have his tales repeated to other listeners, for he begins the story with the assumption that his tales reach beyond his immediate audience: "If you repeat this tale to the White Hussars . . ." (p. 232) is how the story begins. Thus, he uses language, the word, to move out of himself, and his tales reveal his perception of the facts of man's existence.

IV

He holds him with his glittering eye--
The Wedding Guest stood still,
And listens like a three years' child:
The Mariner hath his will.[20]

The Ancient Mariner transfixes the Wedding Guest as much by his power of expression as by his glittering eye. There is a purpose behind his manipulation of language--to reveal the vision of universal love and communitas,[21] a vision he has arrived at after plumbing the very depths of horror. The narrator of the tales has a similar capacity to make language an extension of his vision. Thus his language is at once ambiguous (when he is uncertain of the truth of a situation), explicit (in his moral generalizations), implicit (in the open ended language with which he ends his tales) and mysterious (when he perceives the presence of the indefinable supernatural). Through his powerful use of language, therefore, he mesmerizes the audience into a suspension of disbelief. As with the Ancient Mariner, there is a purpose behind his manipulation of the audience, a purpose which becomes steadily clearer to him as he searches for the truth in human experience and tries to understand it.

The experience of the characters in his tales forms part of the formation of his own vision of truth. His choice of tales is therefore deliberate, each tale requiring the proper moment to be narrated. Tales remembered in the telling of another, are often dismissed as "that's another story," which will be told at some other time. Each of the tales under discussion reveals a little more of human experience to the narrator. As one tale is succeeded by the next, the narrator reveals a combination of courage and honesty which compels him to disclose "the horror." But this revelation is often accompanied by an intuitive understanding of the cause that lies behind the suffering and chaos which lead these individuals to welcome an untimely death. "I choked while I was putting down these things" (p. 23) says the narrator in "Thrown Away," while composing a letter to The Boy's parents, and this might be said of his response to the tragic experiences that he narrates. But then, he "laughed at the grotesqueness of the affair, and the laughter mixed itself up with the choke" (pp. 23-24). However, in a few tales, the hysterical laughter at the absurdity of man's existence dissolves into compassion and a laughter, which, as many critics have noted, has a healing quality.[22]

In some of the tales, while recognising the tragedy which afflicts certain individuals, the narrator accepts solutions provided by society to prevent such tragedies from occurring. Thus, in "Thrown Away," he explains the tragic circumstances which lead to The Boy's death as being unnecessary. According to him, the tragedy could have been avoided if The Boy had not been brought up "under what parents call the 'sheltered life system'" (p. 15). The narrator, therefore, provides his tale with a moral, and, in the process of doing so, reduces the problem of alienation to the relatively simple one of conforming to a set of social "habits." At the same time, he is equivocal in his analysis of The Boy's non-conformity. While he admits that it "was pitiful to watch The Boy knock himself to pieces" (p. 18), he does not provide the concrete circumstances which led The Boy to do so. All he reveals are the outward disasters that afflict The Boy, such as the loss of money in gambling, nervous exhaustion, and the insult offered him by a woman, this last incident being the direct cause (so it seems) of his suicide. The equivocation is deliberate, for even after the death of The Boy, the narrator excuses himself for not revealing the true cause behind his death by stating that it "is much too sacred to put into print" (p. 22). Even if the narrator is aware of the bottomless pit of darkness which destroys The Boy's faith in himself,[23] he is unwilling to admit it. It may be this unwillingness to face the problem of alienation that leads the narrator to blame the tragedy on the external realities of "the sheltered life system," and India.

However, India has nothing to do with The Boy's innate sensitivity, as becomes apparent in the contents of the letter he leaves behind. An awareness of "disgrace," "criminal folly," and "indelible shame" has nothing to do with the subcontinent, but a great deal to do with the state of his mind, which coming to an alien land may have helped worsen. "It was no time for little lies, you will understand" (p. 23) says the narrator, and the biggest lie is fabricating a world view where the problems of the psyche are transferred to the external, indifferent reality of India.

Similarly, in "False Dawn," though on one level the eerie dust-storm does act as a symbol of the chaos among the group, the narrator externalizes the conflict which occurs within Saumarez, and lays the blame for the misunderstanding that takes place on the dust-storm. That the narrator does this subconsciously is evident from his reaction to the storm before Saumarez proposes to the wrong sister. Aware that a fierce dust-storm is about to erupt, he dismisses it as a natural occurrence of no great significance: "A dust-storm, more or less, does no great harm" (p. 46). But, when Saumarez admits to him, "I've proposed to the wrong one" (p. 48), the storm takes on the proportions of a demonic force, and the narrator replies: "More fool you for proposing in a dust-storm" (p. 48). From then on, the narrator vindicates both Saumarez's actions and his own reactions by insisting that the storm was in some way responsible for their foolishness. Thus he states: "I fancy neither of us were ourselves just then. He was shaking as he stood with excitement and I was feeling queer all over with the electricity" (p. 48). He even accounts for his decision to take an active part in settling the affairs of this "misguided world" (p. 52) in similar terms: "It must have been my state of overexcitement that made me so ready to meddle with what did not concern me" (p. 49). Since he seems to be anxious to establish his role as a mere observer, he makes excuses for his obvious desire to create order out of chaos. It is in the midst of his "evil dream," which leads him "across the desolate plain . . . through beds of burnt-down jungle grass . . . with the lightning crackling overhead and a reek like the smell of the pit in my nostrils" (p. 50), that he has a vision of his purpose: "All the world was only the two Copleigh girls, Saumarez and I; ringed in with the lightning and the dark; and the guidance of this misguided world seemed to lie in my hands" (p. 52). But the momentary vision is dismissed as the "Great Pop Picnic," which disappears along with the "dust-storm and the tingle in the hot air," in favour of being "ordinary men and women" (p. 55). However, the desire to create order remains, though the means which the narrator chooses are not going to lead to the correct solution. He believes that conforming to the social habit of sending women to the hills for the hot season would have averted the misunderstanding.

The problem lies, however, not with the approaching "hot weather" or the dust-storm, but with the characters themselves, and the only means of creating order is by transforming the chaos within. The incident itself is a trifling one, yet the narrator gives the impression of its being a much more tragic affair. Though he tries to explain this palpable and yet indefinable sense of tragedy in terms of the cosmic upheaval, he is aware that the tragedy is rooted in the world of man, and not nature. The truth about the perfect, divine communion that is love between man and woman, flashes upon him as a flash of lightning reveals to him the sight of a girl on whose face was the "look . . . which only comes once or twice in a lifetime--when a woman is perfectly happy and the air is full of trumpets and gorgeously coloured fire, and the earth turns into cloud because she loves and is loved" (p. 49). While the very words used to describe the scene are apocalyptic, it is, for the girl, a "false dawn." Such perfect love is unattainable, both for her and for modern man. It is wrong, therefore, to think that her agony--not identifiable with the natural, cosmic upheaval--will pass together with the storm. The narrator seems to realize this, and ends the story with a sensitive identification with the agonised woman: "There is," he states, "a woman's version of this story, but it will never, be written. . . Unless Maud Copleigh cares to try" (p. 53).

The mocking laughter which the narrator exhibits in "Thrown Away" thus gives way to sympathy for mankind in other tales. However, he still adheres to the belief that conforming to rules can prevent tragedy, and this belief dictates his moral stance in "Beyond the Pale," which opens with a generalization: "A man should, whatever happens, keep to his own caste, race and breed. Let the White go to the White and the Black to the Black" (p. 171), and his tale is to be an illustration of this principle. But, if he mocks The Boy for his sensitivity, and Saumarez for his folly, he sympathizes with Trejago, the man who broke the rule. He genuinely tries to understand Trejago's alienation which makes "office work" and calling "on the ladies of the station" so trivial compared with his "dearer, out-of-the-way life" (p. 176). The result, as the narrator is at pains to point out, is tragedy. However, there seems to be a question in his mind whether over-stepping of bounds is responsible for the tragedy, or, and this seems more likely, whether it is because like the rest of his race, Trejago continues to look at things "from a western standpoint" (p. 177). If the second reason is the correct one, the attempt to form a communion with an Indian who is ruled by the proverb "Love heeds not caste nor sleep a broken bed" (p. 171), is doomed to failure. The narrator seems inclined to prefer the second reason. He knows that since the white man can never "lose himself" in love, it is better to "keep to his own caste," as then "whatever trouble falls is in the ordinary course of things--neither sudden, alien, nor unexpected" (p. 171). The vision is admittedly bleak, but here, the "rule" is not seen as the ultimate good, but as the lesser of two evils.

There is, therefore, a change in the narrator's perspective in this tale. Though his analysis of human experience remains truthful, he is not confident that the cause of tragic experience lies merely in actions that defy the code set by society. Yet, he chooses, however shakily, to propagate the necessity of maintaining the habits that sustain society and prevent tragedy because he is unable to suggest any other way. At the same time, there is a hint that if Trejago had not insisted on looking at things "from a western standpoint," there would have been no tragedy.

It is in "The Bisara of Pooree" that the narrator betrays a certain amount of confidence in his role as the "guide" of this "misguided world."[24] His own disillusionment with the artificiality of "civilization," and its precarious attempt to disregard the darker, subliminal areas of man's psyche, makes him comprehend more clearly the mysterious functionings of such areas. Thus, tales that deal with magic and mystery form an important part of his repertoire. In this story, India is seen as a land which has the power to stimulate "belief," which counteracts the isolation of modern European man, who has been divorced from such belief. It is the Englishman "who knew how to believe" who is perceived as being the balanced individual to be emulated. It is because of his powerful, imaginative grasp of reality that the "man who knew how to believe" is able to grasp the knowledge of the cosmic balance of good and evil, which makes a boon sometimes its opposite, a curse. Thus, he "fastened the Bisara of Pooree inside the necklace" of a cart-pony, and "thanked Heaven he was rid of danger" (p. 267). By the end of the tale, the narrator begins to believe, without questioning the rationale behind the belief. He turns instead, with anger to the typical Englishman, saying: "You will say that all this story is made up. Very well. If ever you come across a little, silver, ruby-studded box, seven-eighths of an inch long by three-quarters wide, with a dark brown wooden fish, wrapped in gold cloth inside it, keep it. Keep it for three years, and then you will discover for yourself whether my story is true or false" (p. 268).

The desire to believe the experience of Misquitta leads the narrator to refrain from interpretation in "The Gate of the Hundred Sorrows." "This is no work of mine" he proclaims and consciously accepts the role of the narrator as mere medium, with Misquitta narrating the tale himself. Significantly, the narrator gives the tale a journalistic form, almost as though by doing so he hopes to convince those who do not know how to believe, of the verifiability of the story. Interpretation is kept to a minimum in "By Word of Mouth" as well. If in "Thrown Away" and "False Dawn" he tries to rationalise the tragedy which befalls the protagonists, in "By Word of Mouth" he admits that any one "explanation is false." Knowledge does not necessarily imply total comprehension, as being in India teaches him. Thus he states: ". . . I have lived long enough in this India to know that it is best to know nothing" (p. 318), and presents the story "as it happened."

Indeed, explanations are not necessary, for in the experience of Dumoise lies the evasive truth about the boundlessness of the "Possible." The narrator, therefore, does not feel it incumbent upon himself to provide explanations for the appearance of the ghost of Dumoise's wife, or the untimely death of Dumoise himself. He does hazard a guess at the cause of the tragedy itself, and this time it has nothing to do with social laws. He admits the problem to be one of alienation. "Few people can afford to play Robinson Crusoe anywhere" (p. 319), he states before narrating the story. He also recognizes that the solution to this problem might lie in establishing a community of good-will, for "we are . . . very much dependent on each other's kind offices" (p. 319).

It is a similar alienation which the narrator sees as the cause behind Jelalludin's suicidal attempt to disintegrate into death through the power of alcohol. He has, however, a superior attitude towards the "fallen man," fallen, that is, "from a respectable point of view." As Jelalludin perceptively notes, the narrator maintains "a position in society"(p. 328),[25] which prevents him from touching the depths that Misquitta or Jelalludin touch. Maintaining this position acts as the "veil" which leaves him painfully "ignorant of many things" (p. 328) as Jelalludin states. The latter seems to be the narrator's alter-ego. He has seen and experienced the mystery which the narrator achieves merely through listening to the experience of others. Jelalludin's bluntness in telling him so appears to make the narrator hostile towards him, but it is the truth about himself that Jelalludin reveals to him. Thus, the narrator sees only a "hopeless muddle" in Jelalludin's "monument more enduring than brass," his "one book" (p. 334). But he has learnt enough not to disregard the truth that challenges empirical reality and logic, and his closing statement reveals an implicit acceptance of Jelalludin's mysterious and surrealistic experience. The story ends with the narrator admitting: "I don't want the 'Giant's Robe' to come true in my case" (p. 336).

As has been demonstrated, the vision that is presented in *Plain Tales From the Hills* is often bleak, full of despair, alienation and death. But, whereas in some tales the narrator seems to believe that the solution lies in conforming to the rules and "habits" endorsed by society, in others he seems to believe that there is no simple explanation, no easy solution, for the problem lies in the inescapable fact of the isolation of man. There is a solution, however, a solution that the

Ancient Mariner is aware of, but one he learnt after plumbing the very depths of horror himself. It is in *Life's Handicap* that the narrator includes tales in which he himself confronts the Powers of Darkness. But it is in the next selection under discussion, *Phantom Rickshaw and Other Tales*, that the vision reveals clearly the regions of the horrible, the inexplicable, and the demonic. It is in this selection, too, that the narrator displays an intuitive grasp of knowledge indispensable to the seer, the knowledge of "how souls are made and where the bounds of the Possible are" (p. 318).

NOTES

1. Rudyard Kipling, "The Prayer of Miriam Cohen," in *Rudyard Kipling's Verse* (New York: Doubleday, Doran and Co., 1928), p. 687.

2. Rudyard Kipling, "Thrown Away," in *Plain Tales From the Hills* (London: Macmillan, 1910). This tale was first published in this collection in 1888. *Plain Tales* was first published in 1888, and the first English edition came out in 1890. Of the total number of 40 stories, 29 had appeared in the *Civil and Military Gazette* during the period Nov. 1886-June 1887. The first English edition contained the 40 original stories, but with a revised text. All further references to tales from this collection are to this edition..

3. Rudyard Kipling, "False Dawn," in *Plain Tales* (P.T.). This tale was first published in this collection in 1888.

4. Rudyard Kipling, "The Gate of the Hundred Sorrows," in *P.T.* This tale was first published in the *Civil and Military Gazette* on 26 Sept., 1884.

5. By "modern" I mean belonging to the centuries that followed the decline of religious faith in the Renaissance. In fact, Charles Glicksburg in *The Literature of Nihilism* (Lewisburg: Bucknell U. Press, 1975), states that the age of Enlightenment "undermined the foundations of faith and left a spiritual void that none of the proposed secular remedies could hope to fill" (pp. 120-21). Because of this decline of faith, man, in the last few centuries has been progressively seeing himself as alienated, abandoned by meaning, which had earlier been provided by religion. Thus, death becomes a major problem. Despair at

the inevitability of death is, however, often balanced by the intense desire for the oblivion of death.

6. Glicksburg, in *The Literature of Nihilism*, argues that towards the end of the nineteenth century, "many writers were driven to despair by their feeling of cosmic alienation" (p. 51), and this "new despair rose from a world which gave no room for idealism, illusion or morality whatever" (p. 51). Kipling is a true nihilist when it comes to dealing with this despair that arises out of the horrifying perception of nothingness. But, like the nihilists he believes that there is a "secular future when mankind will establish the Kingdom of Heavan on Earth" (Glicksburg, p. 52).

7. In the other collections under discussion, Kipling tends to include all mankind in this problem of alienation. This, of course, becomes exceedingly clear in the tales he wrote of the first world war.

8. Rudyard Kipling,"Beyond the Pale," in *P.T.*, the tale was first published in this selection. The reference is to page 177.

9. Samuel Beckett, in an essay on Proust, says: "Life is a succession of habits since the individual is a succession of individuals. . . . Habit, then, is the generic term for the countless treaties concluded between the countless subjects that constitute the individuals and their countless correlative objects." Thus, habit acts as a deadener that "chains the dog to his vomit." The periods of transition which separate consecutive adaptations "represent the perilous zones in the life of the individual, dangerous, precarious, painful, mysterious . . . . when for a moment, the boredom of living is replaced by the suffering of being" (p. 110). Thus, if the concept is applied to a collection of individuals, a society, habit defines the collective attitude of the society. The quotation from Beckett is taken from Martin Esslin's *The Theatre of the Absurd* (Garden City: Anchor, 1969).

10. Rudyard Kipling," Wressley of the Foreign office," in *P.T.*, the tale was first published in the *Civil and Military Gazette*, 20 May, 1987.

11. E.M. Forster, *A Passage to India* (Harmondsworth: Penguin, 1936), p. 10.

12. Refer to note 9. These individuals live in perpetual awareness of their condition, unlike the others who allow "habit" to deaden their sensibility.

13. The narrator, by constantly comparing The Boy with animals,

dehumanizes him to a certain extent.

14. It is "divine" contentment because, as McIntosh states, it is a state where "I am as the Gods knowing good and evil, but untouched by either" (p. 331).

15. The "Opium Smoker's Proverb" is given as the epigram to this tale: "If I can attain Heaven for a pice, why should you be envious?" (p. 277)

16. The narrator in "By Word of Mouth " states: "Few people can afford to play Robinson Crusoe anywhere" (p. 319).

17. Rudyard Kipling, "By Word of Mouth," in *P.T.* The tale was first published in the *Civil and Military Gazette*, 10 June, 1887.

18. Kipling has as an epigraph to the "House of Suddhoo" a few lines of verse from his poem "From the Death to the Dawn," and India is described as being,

A stone's throw out on either hand
From that well-ordered road we tread
And all the world is wild and strange:
Churel and Ghoul and Djinn and Sprite
Shall bear us company tonight
For we have reached the Oldest Land
Wherein the Powers of Darkness range. (p. 144)

19. Rudyard Kipling, "To Be Filed for Reference," in *P.T.*, the tale was first published in this collection.

20. S.T. Coleridge, "The Rime of the Ancient Mariner," in *Selected Poetry and Prose of Coleridge*, ed. Donald A. Stauffer (Modern Library, 1981), 13-16.

21. "Communitas" is a term used by Victor Turner in his book *Dramas, Fields and Metaphors* (Ithaca: Cornell U. Press, 1974). He uses it to refer to the best possible form of communication that can exist between men.

22. "Laughter" as a healing agent in Kipling's work, has been discussed by several critics at length. Dobrée's statement is the most representative. In *Rudyard Kipling: Realist and Fabulist* (London: Oxford U. Press, 1967), Dobrée states that "what distinguishes Kipling is the laughter as described by John Davidson, which has been named 'cosmic mirth' by Professor C.A. Bodelsen" (p. 40). He also analyses the various types of laughter in Kipling, "ironic laughter" (p. 39), the

"lighter laughter of social comedy" (p. 39), "laughter of revenge," healing laughter and cosmic laughter.

23. The Major describes it as the "Valley of Shadow."

24. However, the narrator does not exhibit a consistent sense of responsibility towards society as a seer/guide.

25. As a number of modern novelists have revealed, notably Joyce in *Ulysses*, *A Portrait of the Artist as a Young Man*, and "The Dead," realization does not necessarily lead to a change of personality. Habits are far too difficult to break, so that epiphanic moments remain brief illuminations of the truth, but do not change the individual immediately, if at all.

Phantom Rickshaw and Other Tales

I

In the Preface to *Phantom Rickshaw and Other Tales*, Kipling states: "This is not exactly a book of downright ghost stories as the cover makes believe. It is rather a collection of facts that never quite explained themselves."[1] Thus, the dividing line between empirical reality and the reality which defies definition, is deliberately blurred. The term "fact" itself is reduced to denoting mere external, incontrovertible phenomena, such as the fact that "one man insisted upon dying because he believed himself to be haunted; another man either made up a wonderful lie and stuck to it, or visited a very strange place; while the third man was indubitably crucified by some person or persons unknown and gave an extraordinary account of himself."[2] It is with the vision, as it emerges from a study of these facts and experiences which take these characters to the twilight regions of the inexplicable, that this chapter is to be largely concerned. The three tales to be studied in detail are "Phantom Rickshaw," "The Strange Ride of Morrowbie Jukes," and "The Man Who Would Be King" respectively.

In the Preface Kipling reveals the stance which the narrator takes in narrating the tales. In this selection, "facts" do not explain themselves because the narrator's growing interest in the twilight regions of the mind makes him narrate tales that delve deep into the minds of individuals tortured by memories of a horrifying past. This implies an implicit acceptance on the narrator's part as on Kipling's, that the battle ground on which the forces of light and dark, life and death struggle for supremacy is the mind of man. Therefore, the mind can make man divine, as in the case of Shelley's Prometheus, or demonic, as in the case of Marlowe's Faustus, or merely a shadow, as with Eliot's hollow men. Since it is in the mind that the drama of conflict takes place, the reader is allowed to delve into the mind of the character and analyse, as the character himself does the torment of remembered experience. By doing so, both the narrator and the reader peer into the hell in which these individuals find themselves trapped.

The vision itself becomes increasingly difficult to classify, as each individual character's experience acquires a shape that sets it apart from the experience of others. The only common factor in the experience of the protagonists of the three tales, is the effect which the encounter with the inexplicable has on them. The terrifying sense of demonic persecution and incessant torture alienates them from the rest of a disbelieving world. For the latter, these people are "mad," but the so-called madness is a truthful manifestation of the chaos that results from a confrontation with the truth of modern existence--the hell which lies precariously close beneath the superficial layer of rationality. Hell and the dark powers exist both on the microcosmic and macrocosmic levels. Thus, the experience of the protagonists in the "ghost-stories" is inextricably linked with their psychological condition, and the setting, which seems almost an objective correlative to their inner condition, is, most often, exceedingly sinister. No longer is the danger definable in the form of a concrete dust-storm, as in "False Dawn," or a Bisara of Pooree, but contained within vast areas of sand dunes, treacherous quick-sands, landslides and stark, barren mountains which threaten to obliterate man's identity. Madness and death form the inevitable and for the characters who encounter the dark powers. But such madness is the madness of the seer, which as Coleridge warns, the ordinary man rightly fears, for the former has certainly seen into the very truth of being--a knowledge dangerous for men of limited vision.

Although the vision gets increasingly more stark and despairing, the narrator exploits his gift of prophetic insight to reveal the possibility of future redemption for mankind. If in *Plain Tales From the Hills* he merely offers a vision of the horrifying condition of modern man, doomed to suffer, in this selection, he perceives in the horrifying experience positive energy which can save man. This energy is inextricably linked with Christ, the crucified god of love, as a discussion of "The Man Who Would Be King" will elucidate. However, it remains a mere theoretic possibility, and the narrator recognizes it as such.

II

If Miriam Cohen prays, as do the other characters of *Plain Tales From the Hills*, for a "veil" to protect them from seeing "unto madness," the tormented, alienated individuals who figure in *Phantom Rickshaw and Other Tales* know this desire is a dream impossible to realize. The collection opens with an epigram which indicates the futility of cultivating "habits" that act as the "bulkhead" against despair. The epigram is in the form of a prayer to protect man from the already present darkness: "May no ill dream disturb my rest / Nor Powers of Darkness me molest." It is based on the awareness that the dark side of man's soul, inexplicable ill-dreams and the powers of darkness exist and must be believed to exist before they can be dealt with. Thus, Jack Pansay's manuscript in "The Phantom Rickshaw"[3] is a record of the power of ill-dreams--which makes the physical reality of Simla seem fake--to erode the self. As the tale begins, the reader is inveigled into entering the mind of Pansay by way of the revealing manuscript which he is invited to peruse together with the narrator.

That the manuscript holds some terrifying experience which has led to immeasurable torment is evident, for it is the memory of that torment which takes him back to the fateful year he had met, loved and rejected Mrs Keith-Wessington. The past is remembered in terms of fear--its origins, and the revelation of some deep truth that hurts even in the act of remembering. The experience originates, as Jack admits, in his rejection of the lady. "I was the offender," he states, "and I knew it" (p. 6) However, the fear of being trapped in a relationship which he had indulged in merely for amusement, makes Jack vent the force of his hatred on Mrs Keith-Wessington. It is, as he states, possibly "the same instinct . . . which prompts a man to savagely stamp on the spider he has but half-killed" (p. 6). He seems to exult in possessing the power of the predator, and uses it savagely too. Thus, he admits that his replies to the pleadings of the rejected woman "might even have made a man wince," and it "cut the dying woman like the blow of a whip" (p. 8). The quality of mercy is unknown to him and he believes that being "kind" to her would have been a "delusion."

However, as the reader soon becomes aware, guilt afflicts him, even though he refuses to admit it--and in a much more serious manner, since it has been repressed--forcing him towards the horror of persecution by inexplicable fears. As he looks back at the past, the year 1884 comes clearly to his decaying mind as a "confused nightmare wherein light and shade were fantastically intermingled--my courtship of little Kitty Mannering . . . and now and again a vision of a white face flitting by in the rickshaw under the black and white liveries I once watched for so earnestly" (p. 7). His use of the term "vision" reveals the guilt which haunts him, and this vision merges with the actual meetings with Mrs Keith-Wessington. From this moment onwards, Jack's predatory actions and the accompanying guilt cause all the landmarks of his slow degeneration to be firmly etched on his mind. It is not merely the "sodden, dingy pines, the muddy road and the black powder-riven cliffs," witness to his earlier relationship, that torment him, but a "vision" of the "black and white liveries of the *jhampanies*, the yellow-panelled 'rickshaw and Mrs Keith-Wessington's bowed-down golden head" (p. 8) as well.

With the death of Mrs Keith-Wessington, Jack believes that he is at last rid of his past, and the guilt which tortured his mind. This is symbolized in his burning all the correspondence with the ill-fated lady. However, though all external evidence of their relationship is obliterated, the guilt remains to haunt him to his grave. Thus, without realising it, Jack becomes a prey to the forces of darkness within his own soul. He is a prey to ill dreams and it is significant that the first time the "vision" disturbs him is after he has pledged himself to Kitty Mannering by presenting her an engagement ring. At this moment, he hears a voice "apparently at a vast distance" beckoning to him, a voice "he once knew" (p. 11). The "flood of undesirable memories which he tries to destroy by formally contracting himself to Kitty, is upon him. The trap begins to open beneath his feet and what he sees under him is "unutterable horror" and persecution of the self by the vision of "a face from the grave," which, in defiance of "every law of probability, in direct outrage of nature's ordinance" (p.14), seems alive. At this stage, Jack does not seem to realise that his conduct with Mrs Keith-Wessington before her death had been as much an "outrage of Nature's ordinance" as her ghostly appearance.

Jack, the "inside" narrator, recreating his experience, realizes the fact that "from the horrible to the commonplace is but a step" (p. 12) and the line which divides his commonplace courtship of Kitty Mannering, sanctioned by society, from the horrid reality of his guilt-burdened conscience, quickly disappears as the "shadow" of his "first lie" creates a division between Kitty and him. The horrible impinges on the commonplace till "every inch of the Jakko road bore witness to . . . old time walks and talks. The boulders were full of it; the pines sang it aloud overhead; the rain-fed torrents giggled and chuckled over the shameful story, and the wind in my ears chanted the iniquity aloud" (p. 15), or so it seemed to the tortured Jack.

The empirical world recedes further into the background as the "infernal Thing blocking my path in the twilight" becomes somehow the reality. Thus Jack stands and talks the "commonplace of the day for five minutes to the Thing" (p. 18), as he would with the living. Through the shades of the treacherous hill-roads, the vision becomes a guide, preventing Jack and his companion, the doctor, from almost certain death under a landslide of overhanging cliffs. Jack's desperate desire to return to "normal" makes him cling to the doctor's belief that he suffers from "spectral illusion" caused by the "eyes, brain and stomach" (p. 21). But, even the "intoxication" that comes of believing his theory is rudely destroyed by the reappearance of the vision the moment he is beyond the protective walls of the doctor's house.

To the world, Jack's peculiar, horrific experience is the result of "epileptic fits" (p. 26), and increasingly, he becomes part of the ghostly world and an outsider to the society of the living. The process of exploring "the lowest circles of the Inferno" on "earth" begins, and the signs of an incipient disintegration sets in. His limited self, confined by the restraints of a society that demands a rational explanation of all irrational experience, watches his other, more real and yet more dangerous self. "I myself was watching myself faltering through the dark labyrinths of doubt, misery and utter despair" (p. 27). This fatal division is never quite overcome; wholeness of self has been fragmented, so that even when the two selves join, the one predominates over the other, as Jack despairingly admits: "Then my two selves joined, and it was only I (half-crazed, devil-driven I) that tossed in my bed" (p. 27). Thus, while a part of him clings desperately to the doctor's theory, the other part begins to question the "diseased inner self" (p. 29).

The sense of being trapped in an irrevocable situation leaves Jack with the despairing belief that the only course left open to him is to surrender himself to the powers of darkness till the death "I hope and pray daily for" and "dread by night" overtakes him. With his surrender, the twilight region of the supernatural becomes reality and light, whereas the living appear shadowy and elusive, so that "it seemed that the rickshaw and I were the only realities in a world of shadow; that Kitty was a ghost; that Mannering, Heatherley and all the men and women I knew were all ghosts; and the great, grey hills themselves but vain shadows devised to torture me" (p. 29). This phase of his "sickness," as he terms it, is understandably the most "tormenting," for it reverses all accepted notion of reality, which he discovers no longer apply to him. Thus, his segregation from society, whose notions of reality necessitate the expulsion of Jack from its midst, is sealed. Since reality is not what he, as part of the society of man believed it to be, he attempts to understand the nature of reality as his bizarre experience reveals it to him. But, truth seems to elude his understanding and it is to Mrs Keith-Wessington that he appears "for pity's sake" to reveal to him "what it all means" (p. 30).

The Truth that the dead woman reveals to him is not divulged to the narrator or the reader. After the revelation, however, Jack seems to find it easier to accept his no-man's-land existence. Hunger for "the society of my kind" is balanced by an equally strong desire to associate with the dead, and he feels "vaguely unhappy" when he has been separated too long from his "ghostly companion" (p. 32). This awareness of the schism in his emotional, intellectural and psychological self leads him to the dull and numbing wonder that "the Seen and the Unseen should mingle so strangely on this earth to hound one poor soul to its grave" (p. 33).

However, Jack's terrifying agony is more truthful for recognising that the mysterious reality of the seen and unseen can never be fully explained, but must be faced. The society which surrounds him is truly ghostly, for it chooses to disregard the inexplicable mystery of life by denying its existence. Thus, strange behaviour is, according to this society, the result of insanity or "epileptic fits," as in Jack's case. Jack's death is therefore inevitable. Since his agony is not understood by those of his "own kind," he cannot expect to get the sort of succour he requires, and, on the other hand, the demonic world created by guilt demands, according to him, his death.

It is with this death-wish that Jack ends his story. The relative peace which follows is a result of his attempt to recreate his past and penetrate the chaotic experience which has left him shattered. As he relives his experience in memory, he seems to believe that he has committed a grave injustice for which he has had to pay heavily with his sanity. What form vengeance, nemesis, or the powers of darkness will take in the future, he is not sure, but his imagination conjures images, not of peace, but of eternal entrapment. To his agonised questions:

"Shall I return to my old lost allegiance in the next world, or shall I meet Agnes, loathing her and bound to her side through all eternity ? Shall we two hover over the scene of our lives till the end of Time ?" (p. 34), no one presumes to offer an answer, not even the narrator, for there are no answers, only questions. Jack dies with a gesture that shows that he has learnt the answer to one question, for he has learnt the value of "pity." If earlier he believed it would have been a "delusion" to be "kind" to Mrs Keith-Wessington, he now requests the reader to "pity" the dead woman, for "as surely as ever woman was killed by man, I killed Mrs Wessington" (p. 34). Maybe, as with the Ancient Mariner, this last gesture of altruism will free Jack from the torment and entrapment which he envisages extending beyond death into infinity.

If Jack imagines himself trapped for infinity, Jukes, the protagonist of "The Strange Ride of Morrowbie Jukes,"[4] experiences the horror of being trapped in death while still alive. Though the epigram is a proverb that states: "Alive or dead--there is no other way" (p. 35), it is the misfortune of characters such as Jack Pansay and Jukes to discover the horrifying world which exists midway between these two extremes of life and death. Society and the concerns of the empirical world are forgotten as the reader penetrates the mind of Morrowbie Jukes to discover, once again, the immense torment which aligns him with Pansay. The past crystallizes into one particular night, the night of the twenty-third of December, 1884. Jukes remembers it being an eerie time--a combination of the "full moon" and the frenetic "baying of dogs." Jukes responds to the numinous mood in a strange manner. He is suddenly seized with a desire to slaughter "one huge black and white beast who had been foremost in song and first in flight throughout the night" (p. 37).

It is the desire for slaughter--the desire of a predator to assert mastery over his prey--that sets off a chain of reactions which Jukes, ironically enough, seems unable to prevent. "Delirium," a condition in which revelations are common, releases his subconscious mind which takes control over the rational sense that normally dictates his actions as an ordinary Civil Engineer. (It is appropriate therefore, that his "ride" takes place at night--a time of uncertainty and mystery). Jukes is himself perplexed at his behaviour and at his firm conviction that his "best plan would be to ride him down in the open and finish him off with a hog-spear" (p. 37), and accounts for the ludicrousness of the idea by asserting that "this of course, was merely the semi-delirious notion of a fever patient" (p. 37). But, it seems to be the dim sense of the excitement which precedes a revelation, that spurs him on, so that once the ride has begun, "I had almost forgotten why it was that I had taken horse and hog-spear" (p. 37). Time loses its impact as the rider and horse streak over the "smooth sandy soil" (p. 37), towards the revelation awaiting them beyond the "unseen slope" (p. 38).

Once Jukes enters the strange world, as undefined as the world of the camp is defined, he surrenders utterly the practical reality that rules his existence in the camp. Freeing himself from the bonds of rationality, Jukes finds himself doing exactly the same as the dogs--baying at the moon, but in human fashion. He stands "upright" in his "stirrups" and brandishes his "hog-spear at the great white moon that looked down so calmly" on his "mad gallop" (p. 38). Thus, as with Jack Pansay, from being the predator, intent on slaughtering his prey, Jukes metamorphoses into the hunted, a victim of his own cruelty (literally, his cruel desire to slaughter leads him to his encounter with death-in-life). It is not surprising that when Jukes recovers his consciousness, he awakens to the knowledge of being trapped beyond the "unseen slope,"--a place to which the logic and consciousness of the living does not apply. The recovery of his empirical senses leads Jukes to apply the principles of the normal world to his situation, which dictates escape. But, such principles are not effective in this world. He is truly trapped, "dead and buried," as Gunga Das mocks, while physically alive. Escape is impossible with sand dunes on one side, an immense tract of quicksand on another, and a river constantly guarded by mysterious people on the third. All attempts leave Jukes baffled, "bleeding," suffering an "agony of spirit" and terrified of eternal entrapment. But while Jukes is terrified of the mystery which surrounds this world, he never questions or probes within the self to analyse the possible reasons behind his presence in this trap. The natives, with whom he shares this living grace, have an explanation--however strange--to offer for their presence. Gunga Das informs Jukes that "if you die at home and do not die when you come to the ghat to be burnt, you come here" (p. 43). But, Jukes not being a Hindu, has no such explanation to offer. His presence can be accounted for only in psychological terms. He is part of the mysterious society that "ordains" and now, by a curious reversal of fate, has been reduced to being the prey of such a society. Thus, instead of giving the orders, Jukes is forced to obey Gunga Das's commands. Even living in such dire conditions does not divest Jukes of his innate sense of superiority (as part of society that ordains), and it galls him bitterly when he is unable to prevent the "natives" from trampling over his body, for as he states, "I have been accustomed to a certain amount of civility from my inferiors" (p. 41).

Thus, instead of analysing his experience--which would have led him to realise that he was no different from his fellow sufferers--Jukes creates the only structure he understands, the system of coercion and domination. He forces his "inferiors" to submit by threatening them with "the only punishment I had it in my power to inflict--sudden and violent death" (p. 54). However, his attempt to act "God" is parodied by his own situation, one of submission to just such a demonic power, and it is in the hours of darkness that he is mocked by visions of an "amphi-theatre . . . filled with legions of unclean devils . . . hooping up from the shoals below" (p. 55).

It is only a "native's" love and pity for his master that saves Jukes from a condition worse than death. Yet, Jukes does not seem to have learnt the value of pity for the suffering in mankind. As the narrator comments, he is always aware of the "indignity" he had to suffer, and it is the memory of his loss of dignity which seems to cause him more anguish than the terrifying thought of having been trapped in the condition of death-in-life. If Jack narrates his experience to share his torment with others and to beg pity of the reader for all tortured souls, Jukes's sole motive in publishing his story is to trace the identity of the other Englishman who had the misfortune of falling into the same trap. He returns to life more dead than living, not having questioned the "meaning" of it all. Once he is back in the world of the living, he does not even make an attempt to save the others who continue to suffer the fate which he has been spared. He is accepted back into society precisely because he does not pose threatening questions such as Jack does just before his death. What he does share with Jack, Dravot and Carnehan, the protagonists of "The Man Who Would Be King," is the agony of persecution of the self, which he tries to silence by refusing to ask the fundamental question--why he was vouchsafed a vision of unspeakable horror. Thus he justifies his desire to revive the memory of his experience by giving as his reason the attempt to "name" and place the dead Englishman by locating his family. In reality, it makes no difference to the dead man whether he is placed among the living or not, but Jukes seems to have lost his own identity by suppressing the knowledge of the evil that is part of his character in favour of a social identity which sanctions and approves his predatory actions.

III

"The Man Who Would Be King"[5] is clearly one of Kipling's most brilliant tales and presents the vision of truth in the tragic experience of Dravot and Carnehan, who seem to be "everyman" in one sense of the term, in that they are on a quest for selfhood.[6] The tale depends for its success on the symbolic patterns that form the essence of the experience of these two characters. Like Alice in *Through the Looking Glass*, and countless other heroes in quest of selfhood, kingship is envisaged as being the culminating point of their journey. "We are going away to be kings" states Carnehan, and Dravot adds, "Kings in our own right" (p. 81). The desire to become kings is not merely a desire to gain social and political supremacy, but to attain perfection of the self. Thus, Carnehan's reason for leaving India is based on the desire to realise his own self apart from the collective identity which the British in India allow. According to him, "You can't lift a spade, nor a chip of rock, nor look for oil, nor anything like that without all the Government saying--'Leave it alone and let us govern.' Therefore, such as it is, we will let it alone, and go away to some other place where a man isn't crowded and can come to his own. (p. 81). Going to the remote, almost mythical Kafiristan is, from their point of view, the only action they can take in order to attain their ideal of selfhood.

The metaphor of kingship suggests only part of the ideal to be attained. The other informing metaphor in this tale is based on the Christian myth of the brotherhood of man, and thus the epigram to the tale runs: "Brother to a Prince and fellow to a beggar if he be found worthy." As Paul Fussell states, the epigram is strikingly similar to a poem Kipling wrote for a Masonic Banquet called "Banquet Night," and he quotes a few of the lines: " . . . once in so often the messenger brings / Solomon's mandate: 'Forget these things ! / Brother to Beggars and Fellow to Kings / Companion of Princes--forget these things !" Fussell provides quite a convincing analysis of the impact freemasonry had on Kipling's vision in this tale. It is one of the ideal systems, as its fundamental principles are those of the liberal humanist, which Kipling certainly was. Thus, Fussell states that the fellowship of freemasons emphasized "universal brotherhood" and the epigram bears this out. But, he believes that "The Man Who Would Be King" issues from "a young mind excited by Masonic symbolism and Masonic ethical precepts."[8] Far from being a mere exposition of Masonic principles, the story welds the two contraries which lead to the redemption of man--theoretically if not in actuality, the contraries of selfhood and the Keatsian negative capability. Thus, Kipling uses the Masonic creed as an abstract philosophy which, if followed in practice, may have the effect of changing the chaos behind the "veil" into joy.

In the experience of Dravot and Carnehan this idea is not realised, however, and the attempt to attain it results in tragedy. At the moment of supreme realization, when Dravot comes closest to achieving perfection, he goes plummeting down to his death. The true Christ-King, Carnehan, a supreme example of the man who has an imperfect but sacred understanding of the self, besides possessing the negative capability which makes him "brother" to a King and a beggar, when Dravot is both the former and the latter, is crucified, the sacrificial victim of a world in the throes of the madness of cruelty. In order to comprehend the nature of the vision as it is revealed in the experience of these two characters, it is necessary to analyse their movement or journey from the relative freedom of tramps to the entrapment of kings. As with Jack Pansay and Morrowbie Jukes, they begin their journey as predators and end as prey. However, Carnehan and Dravot consciously embark on their quest, whereas the other two are more or less forced into the fatal encounter with the dark powers.

The quest originates in a contract which binds both Carnehan and Dravot together in a relationship of equality, for "me and you will settle this matter together: that is, to be Kings of Kafiristan" (p. 85) states Carnehan in the contract. Besides, both are to abstain from indulging in "Women" and "Liquor." As all the contracts signed by characters in literary works show, any attempt to violate it means self-annihilation. Marlowe's Doctor Faustus veers towards violating the infernal pact with the devil, but the premonitory fear of the consequences prevents him. A contract has to be honoured, and thus Faustus is truly damned forever. Carnehan is aware of the inviolacy of a contract. In fact, he displays it for the narrator as the ultimate proof of the seriousness of their venture, for, "do you think that we would sign a contract like that unless we was in earnest ?" (p. 85)

However, the path towards immortality (Dravot intends becoming the "thirty-third idol" of Kafiristan), is extremely dangerous. According to Mircea Eliade, temples are "sacred" as they symbolise "absolute reality" and "absolute truth,"[9] and Dravot literally establishes himself in this sacred region once he becomes king. But, the "road is arduous, fraught with perils, because it is, in fact, a rite of passage from the profane to the sacred, from the ephemeral and illusory to reality and eternity, from death to life, from man to divinity."[10] Thus, it is symbolic that Dravot and Carnehan should choose the guise of fakirs, holy men who have supposedly gained knowledge of this absolute reality and are therefore under the protection of God. Their destination is the sacred space of Kingship (that is, the attainment of self-hood) and with it the sacred temple as well (that is, the loss of the ego). The journey they must undertake in order to attain their goal is dangerous. But, as the whirligigs and toys they carry with them hide a darker, more destructive reality--in the form of weapons, the guise of fakirs and the ambitious desire to attain the status of "idols," hides a reality much more dangerous than is apparent to them at the moment when they begin their journey. To Dravot, for example, imitating a fakir and offering blessings is just an act to be executed with perfection. He even childishly demands applause of the narrator, for "didn't I do that talk neat ?" (p. 88)

Play gives way to the rigours of the journey and, as they make progress towards their destination, even the physical terrain offers resistance. "The country was mountainous and the mules were most contrary and the inhabitants was dispersed and solitary" (p. 94) states Carnehan. Physical hardship is not all they have to contend with. Dravot in self-defence commits homicide without a qualm of conscience, and this ability to kill men like cattle makes him king. Meeting two warring tribes, by chance, Dravot seizes the opportunity to achieve his goal and shoots at the larger tribe, "picking them off at all ranges, up and down the valley" (p. 94) as Carnehan relates, and establishes himself king of the amazed natives of the smaller tribe. To Dravot, therefore, Kingship means political and social sovereignty, to be gained by force, if necessary. Thus, his first act as king is to shoot above the heads of his newly acquired tribe, and as Carnehan states, "they all fall down flat" (p. 45) out of fear. It is interesting to note that Carnehan never includes himself in any of the honours and is quite content with merely carrying out the orders given by Dravot. Even while narrating his tale, he makes it quite clear that "I wasn't King. Dravot he was the King" (p. 96).

Dravot establishes himself by the "side of old Imbra" in the sacred temple, while the people come and worship in accordance with "Dravot's order." That he sees himself similar to the god of the Old Testament is evident. In fact, he even uses Biblical language in ordering his subjects to work: "Go and dig the land, and be fruitful and multiply" (p. 97).[11] Kingship, then, far from being a divine realization of the self, becomes merely a means of acquiring social and political immortality which has its basis in bloodshed and tyranny. By making himself omnipotent in political terms, Dravot hopes to reach the status of the revered and immortal god of the natives, Imbra. He interprets a religious power which Imbra has, in terms of a political and temporal one. Thus, by creating what Eliade terms a "settlement"[12] out of what he considers to be chaos, he hopes to equal the original act of creation. That this interpretation of Kingship and Divinity is erroneous and dangerous is evident from Carnehan's desire to dissociate himself from the political head of Kafiristan that is the king.

It is not long before Dravot follows up his victories with a coronation and appears in front of Carnehan, a king with a "great gold crown on his head" and a "tail of hundreds of men" (p. 100). His desire has been fulfilled with his coronation. In order to transform this political omnipotence into a religious one, Dravot pronounces himself a "God and Grand-Master of the Craft" (p. 100). Carnehan, on the other hand, sees beyond the blinding light of the crown. To him, the crown is "too small and too heavy," as it is for Alice when she finally becomes a queen. But, the latter might have said with Carnehan, "I wore it for the glory." The sense of confinement, however, does not leave him. In fact, he describes the crown in terms of a constricting band of "five pound weight" which feels like a "hoop of barrel" (p. 101). Carnehan realizes that Kingship is not as simple as it appears to be. This realization is further confirmed in the "amazing miracle" that takes place after the coronation--"The Master's Mark" on the stone of Imbra is discovered to be the same as the one on "Dravot's apron" (p. 103). But, whereas Carnehan, struck with wonder, tends to see in this revelation the gleam of a little understood mystical process, to Dravot the mark is just a mark and nothing else. Instead of questing further into the "meaning" of the miracle, Dravot settles down to the process of accumulating earthly power and omnipotence. He creates a hierarchy of priests, with himself as the equivalent of the immortal Imbra.

Having established himself among the pantheon of gods, Dravot acts in a way that neither Imbra, nor the other gods have ever done or ever will do since the form in which they appear to human beings is that of lifeless stones. Since he is not removed from the processes of life and death, Dravot cannot achieve immortality merely by sitting by the side of stone idols. So, he looks for immortalty in his very humanity. It is through his "heir" that he will live. His desire to avail himself of a "wife" appalls Carnehan, for it means breaking the contract. Having transformed his political powers into immortality sanctified by religion, his desire to have sexual intercourse with one of his "kind" reverses the whole process, for the gods do not mate with human beings. Thus, Dravot's desire to achieve immortality leads to his death. His tyrannical insistence on possessing a wife divests him of his precarious Kingship built on political domination. The revelation of his humanity--in the form of blood--results in a dirge-like chant by the horrified people of Kafiristan: "Neither God nor Devil, but a man !" (p. 114) At the same time, this loss of social and political power leads him to achieve self-realization, thus making him a true king for the eternity of a split second. His blood must nevertheless be shed because he has no signs of divinity to show the crowd. Though he is a prey to the whims of the crowd, the realization that "it's my blasted nonsense that has brought you to this" (p. 117), and his fearless acceptance of death makes him the victor, for he has conquered himself. If, before death, Christ begged forgiveness for mankind, Dravot pleads with Carnehan to forgive him, for he knew not what he did. Finally, he goes plummeting into the abyss which he had hoped to conquer, whirling like the whirligigs with which he had set out to conquer.

It is Peachey for whom is reserved the torture and horror which afflicts Jack and Jukes. In his narration of the agony of his experience, he reveals a sensitive awareness of the tragic overtones of their experiment with Kingship. In fact, it has divested him of all sense of personal identity. He constantly refers to himself in the third person, as though aware of himself as several persons--wholeness fragmented into madness. At times, Carnehan and Dravot merge in his mind and suffer a common death, whereas at other times, he remembers that Carnehan was not allowed to die, but was saved for a more bitter end: "See what they did to Peachey between two pine trees ? They crucified him sir, as Peachey's hands will show. They used wooden pegs for his hands and his feet; and he didn't die. He hung there and screamed, and they took him down next day.... They took him down--poor old Peachey that hadn't done them any... " (p. 119) and the sentence trails off into the piteous lamentation of a bewildered child.

It is Carnehan's implicit faith in the bond between him and Dravot that keeps him alive on his long journey back to India. As he says, "Peachey came home in about a year, begging along the roads, quite safe; for Daniel Dravot he walked before him and said: 'Come along Peachey. Its a big thing we're doing.' The mountains they danced at night and the mountains they tried to fall on Peachey's head, but Dan, he held up his hand, and Peachey came along, bent double. He never let go of Dan's hand, and he never let go of Dan's head" (p. 120), and he reveals the shrunken head of the erstwhile king. The agonising experience has taken its toll as his refusal to let go of Dan's withered head shows. Since time seems to have lost its linearity, his tale is exceedingly fragmented, linked together only by the emotional response that the memory of his experience arouses. Thus he connects the superficial success with the darker and deeper tragedy that took place. For example, he describes Dravot's fall from the bridge in terms of a "penny whirligig that you can sell to the Amir" (p. 93). The linking of the two, death with the whirligig, is a realization of the earlier jocular association of the two.[13] It is only by maintaining the unspoken contact with another human being that Carnehan is able to retain enough sanity to narrate his experience, and his narration is punctuated with the plea: "Keep looking at me, or maybe my words will go all to pieces. Keep looking at me in my eyes and don't say anything." (p. 92)

After he completes his tale, like Jack Pansay, he dies, but not before he reveals himself to be a true seer, rejected by the world which desires safety from just such an experience. He is classified as being "mad" and the narrator takes him to the nearest "missionary" for eventual transfer to the "asylum" (p. 121). His madness is, however, the result of an apocalyptic clarity of vision and he dies singing a song which indicates the depth of his understanding of the tragedy which it is man's lot to experience. The song is his interpretation of the suffering of Christ, the archetypal sufferer:

> The Son of Man goes forth to war
> A golden crown to gain;
> His blood-red banner streams afar--
> Who follows in his train ?
>
> (p. 121)

The lines are taken from a hymn by Reginal Weber, and the first line of the hymn is slightly different: "The Son of God goes forth to war."[14] Thus, Carnehan in his rendering of the hymn, instinctively places Christ as the first in line of human suffering--blood that is shed for the good of all mankind.[15] The imagery links both Dravot, whose "red" blood is shed to prove his humanity and whose beard is always referred to as being "red," as well as Carnehan himself with Christ as the latter "follows in his train." It is in this moment of "madness" that Carnehan achieves what he had originally set out to attain--to "come to his own." The significance of his sacrificial crucifixion is not comprehended by a society of limited vision, and in the eyes of the "newsworld," he is a lunatic that died of "sunstroke." The reader knows better and is given as proof, an indication of the presence of supernatural forces within him, for, the head which Carnehan refused to part with in life, disappears with him into the unknown. The mystery of the resurrection is retained and with it some hope for mankind, even if it is a hope that mankind is not even aware of.

The experience of all the characters in the three "ghost-stories" therefore, reveals horror--but a horror which is peculiar to each of them. Their inability to fully fathom the nature of their experience baffles them, and finally leads to death. None of them are able to see a way out of their torment, except for Carnehan, and even he loses his sanity in the process. It is not only for himself that he laments, but for all men who have been "crucified" literally or metaphorically. It is the narrator who reveals an understanding of Carnehan's half revealed vision, and the first indication of this is his insistence on the necessity of believing the tragic experiences which he chooses to narrate.

IV

The narrator of *Phantom Rickshaw and Other Tales* seems to be quite clearly identical with Kipling, for both insist on the importance of "belief." If Kipling states in the Preface that he, the story-teller, took the tales on trust, the narrator does likewise, and both enjoin the reader to believe. The partial disbelief and irony which characterized the narration of some of the tales in *Plain Tales From the Hills*, is not in evidence, nor does the narrator suggest the social formula as a solution to man's psychological problems. In "Wressley of the Foreign Office,"[16] he states: "If men had not this delusion as to the ultra importance of their own particular employment, I suppose that they would sit down and kill themselves. But their weakness is wearisome, particularly when the listener knows that he himself commits exactly the same sin" (p. 235). The latter half of the statement is important as it indicates the narrator's disillusionment with social solutions to the problems which face modern man. In all the "ghost-stories," society appears merely as a part of the memories which the characters revive in narrating their experiences.

It is important to remember that the narrator chooses the tales he narrates. It becomes clear that his intention is to carry his readers, equipped with the essential quality of belief, with him into the tortured minds of his characters. No judgement is passed on them, except for the judgement which they themselves pass on their own actions of the past. This seems to follow from his implicit and unshaken belief in the verifiability of the experiences of the protagonists. With belief comes acceptance of the vision. Thus, in "Phantom Rickshaw," the narrator is clearly not interested in the moral of the story, and less so in revealing his own reaction, which becomes irrelevant to the revelation of the vision itself. All he permits himself to state is that "Men occasionally break down and become as mixed as the metaphors in this sentence" (p. 2). He presents, however, the explanation which society offers for Jack Pansay's condition in Dr. Heatherley's terms: "Overwork started his illness, kept in alight and killed him, poor devil. Write him off to the system--one man to take the work of two and a half men" (p. 3). Almost casually, the narrator adds: "I do not believe this," and goes on to provide the reader with Jack's version of the "affair" in the form of the latter's manuscript. As in "The Strange Ride of Morrowbie Jukes," he provides both the overly rational and reductive point of view and the more "hag-ridden one" and leaves it to the reader to believe whichever one he wants. The narrator is clear, however, about his own stance and has a theory that "there was a crack in Pansay's head and a little bit of the dark world came through and pressed him to death" (p. 3). The theory is based on the belief that the problems lie with Pansay's head, and its conflict with the "dark world." At the same time, he does not provide any definitions or explanations for the events that take place. He is concerned with finding a way to lessen the pain and torture of the "hag-ridden" man. Thus he suggests to the latter that "he should write out the whole affair from beginning to end, knowing that ink might assist him to ease his mind," and he adds: "this also is Literature" (p. 3). So, though the conflict with the dark powers is recognised as being inevitable, the narrator tries to suggest a way of relieving the pain.

Similarly, it is the mind of Morrowbie Jukes which fascinates the narrator, and he believes in the verifiability of Jukes's experience. "I do not see why Jukes' tale should not be true" (p. 35) he argues with the invisible but ever-present disbeliever. He is aware that the experience of such characters forms "traps" for them, traps from which they are unable to escape, and does not pass any judgement on Jukes. He is merely interested in establishing the fact that "there is, as conjurors say, no deception about this tale" (p. 35). In other words, he affirms Kipling's statement in the Preface that the "book is a collection of facts that never quite explained themselves," and that conjuring is not to be associated with the fantastic. In "My Own True Ghost Story" he explains this idea of higher reality more fully. The imagination he believes to be that quality which creates truth out of reality. Thus, an ordinary evening spent in a spooky "dak-bungalow" which is the sort "to make a man think of every single one of his past sins and of all the others that he intended to commit if he lived" (p. 128), can make of rattling windows and doors a billiards game played by the unquiet dead.

In "The Man Who Would Be King" the narrator becomes a participant in the action and narrates the story himself. He dons the mask of a naive narrator, in sharp contrast to his firm understanding stance in the other stories. The naiveté is a deliberate pose and indicates the exact opposite, but he needs to preserve this mask in order to expose the one-dimensional quality of empirical realism, which is perfectly symbolised in the world of journalism (to which he belongs). He begins the tale with what seems to be an extremely naive statement ridiculing his aspiration to become a "king" for, "if I want a crown I must go hunt it for myself" (p. 69) and his story is an explanation of why this is so.

In recalling his experience, the narrator's memory takes him back to the day he met Carnehan, the day that saw the "beginning of everything." Increasingly, he senses a wide gap between his ordinary "respectable" business where there are no "kings and no incidents except the daily manufacture of a newspaper" (p. 76), and the vagabond, mysterious existence of Dravot and Carnehan. The narrator, however, jeers at the "news" that the two give him of their desire to become kings. This "news" goes beyond the newspaper, map and even the encyclopedia they look up, for it has to do with the evolution of the self. The whole idea seems not only absurd but a death-wish to the narrator for the land beyond the mountains, being unknown, is associated with barbarians and death. While Dravot and Peachey proceed to face the challenge of the unknown, the narrator continues with his hollow routine, till memory of the mad adventurers fades into the trivial acts of "real kings."

The cycle comes to an end three years later, and once again, the narrator is aware of a "strained waiting for something to be telegraphed from the other side of the world" (p. 90). He is not disappointed, for "news" comes literally from the "other side of the world,"--an area beyond the comprehension of the world of news. But this time, the narrator discards the guise of the naive narrator and seems to be convinced of the value of the news, even though it is not the sort that will make the headlines. His interest in the potential news makes him urge Carnehan to "tell me all your can recollect of everything from beginning to end" (p. 92). In discarding his naiveté and displaying belief at this moment, the narrator indicates the necessity for this very naiveté at the beginning of the tale. It is because of his earlier belief in the efficacy of the empirically based news world, that the obverse now becomes apparent and it is revealed for what it is--an extremely limited and hence false representation of reality.

As Carnehan reaches the end of his tale, there is no doubt in the narrator's mind of the truth of the experience which the former has just related. Unfortunately, he does not have any explanations to offer for the mysteriousness of the events outlined by Carnehan, or the disappearance of Dravot's head. The "matter rests" in mystery. His whole acquaintanceship with them, however, appears to have revealed to him the capacity--within each individual--to attain the state of Kingship. But the definition of the term has changed and no longer means the state of political and social power of royalty which makes the headlines in the newspaper.

It is appropriate at this stage to inquire why Kipling considers the question of "belief" to be so central to a proper understanding of the tales in this selection. It is because of his ability to believe that the narrator is able (as has just been proved), to discard the modern empiricist's view of reality and move towards the search for a higher, more imaginative reality. Thus,. he offers these tales to the reader, because all the characters are involved in similar quests for "the meaning of it all," and if they want a crown for themselves, they must--as they do--go "search" for it themselves, as must the narrator. It is in *Life's Handicap, Being Stories of Mine Own People* that the narrator records his own "search," but even in this collection, the search forces him to face the horrors of the dark world through the experience of his characters. A brief glimpse of the joy promised to man (in "The Man Who Would Be King"), however, prevents the vision from deteriorating into the morbid realism of the Naturalists. A brief reference to the narrator's stance in "Wressley of the Foreign Office" will make this clear, as in Wressley's tragic experience, the narrator sees the parable of Christ's love exemplified. It is the power of love, which, according to the narrator, makes Wressley a true poet, even if only for a short while: "Because this sudden and new light of love was upon him, he turned those dry bones of history and dirty records of misdeed into things to weep or to laugh as he pleased. His heart and soul were at the end of his pen, and they got into the ink . . . and his book was a Book. He had his vast special knowledge, so to speak, but the spirit, the woven-in-human touch, the poetry and the power of the output were beyond all special knowledge" (p. 239).

If love is a quantity attainable by all, even a simple historian, it is capable of breaking through the alienation and disintegration of man. Unfortunately, as with Wressley, it is an illusion extremely shortlived. Yet, the quest is definitely towards the positive universe it defines even though the chaos and darkness of individual and societal hell has to be faced before it can be achieved. *Life's Handicap* begins with a quotation which indicates the direction that Kipling's vision was taking in the last decade of the eighteenth century: "I met a hundred men on the road to Delhi and they were all my brothers."[17] The significant words "brother" and "road" capture the main concerns of the short stories in this collection. Most of them are based on the pattern of the quest, the "road" on which thousands move towards death, and since all of mankind is caught in the same trap of life and death, all distinctions of colour, caste and creed give way to the universal oneness which finds linguistic approximation in the expression "brother."

NOTES

1. Rudyard Kipling, *The Phantom Rickshaw and Other Tales* (New York: A.L.Burt, 1900). This collection was originally published in 1888 and contained four stories, "The Phantom Rickshaw," "The Strange Ride of Morrowbie Jukes," "My Own True Ghost Story," and "The Man Who Would Be King." The first English edition came out in 1890. All further references to the short stories of this collection are to this edition.

2. Preface to *The Phantom Rickshaw and Other Tales*.

3. "The Phantom Rickshaw" was first published in *Quartette* in 1885.

4. "The Strange Ride of Morrowbie Jukes" was first published in *Quartette* in 1885.

5. "The Man Who Would Be King" first appeared in *The Phantom Rickshaw and Other Tales*.

6. The desire to become "Kings" is an indication of the nature of their quest. Kingship is a symbol of having attained a level of grace above that of common humanity, and thus the King is revered as the intermediary between God and man, and he confers the state of grace on his subjects, raising them from the imperfections of fallen man to the state of grace.

7. Paul Fussell Jr., "Irony, Freemasonry, and Humane Ethics in Kipling's 'The Man Who Would Be King,'" *ELH*, 25 (1958), p. 225. All

references to Fussell's article are to this publication.

8. Ibid., p. 228.

9. Mircea Eliade, *The Myth of the Eternal Return* (London: Routledge and Kegan Paul, 1955), p.17. All further references are to this book and edition.

10. Ibid., p.18.

11. In *Genesis*, God blesses all living creatures, saying: "Be fruitful and multiply, and fill the waters in the seas, and let fowl multiply in the earth." (*Genesis*, I:22)

12. Eliade states: "Settlement in a new unknown, uncultivated country is equivalent to an act of creation . . . the transformation of chaos into cosmos by the divine act of creation" (p. 10).

13. Fussell has noted this association of the whirligigs and Carnehan's use of the term to describe Dravot's fall from the bridge to death (p. 223).

14. The hymn from which these lines have been taken has been noted by Fussell, (p. 229).

15. The direct correlation between Carnehan and Christ is extremely interesting especially as Christ is, for many modern philosophers, the archetypal image of "unjust execution," as Patrick Grant terms it in his book *Six Modern Authors and Problems of Belief* (London: Macmillan, 1979), p.12. He goes on to say that "all unjust executions, whether of Jesus or the men . . . at Auschwitz, have in common, that they are irreducibly scandalous and the cross remains the only adequate Christian means of approaching them (p. 12). The cross therefore, serves as a reminder of actual, physical agony which religion ritualizes into symbol, the actual agony being submerged in the ritual. It is this agony that is clearly brought out in Carnehan's memory of his crucifixion.

16. This tale first appeared in *Plain Tales From the Hills*.

17. Rudyard Kipling, *Life's Handicap, Being Stories of Mine Own People* (New York: Macmillan, 1896). The reference is to the epigram on the title page. The first English edition of the text came out in 1891 as did the first American edition.

Life's Handicap, Being Stories of Mine Own People

I

In *Life's Handicap*, most of the tales are structures around death, which assumes horrifying proportions.[1] Far from being the welcome end to a long and fulfilled life, it is seen as the inexplicable and dreaded terminating factor of young and old alike. In cholera and the season with which it is associated--the Hot Season--Kipling finds the perfect symbol of the destructiveness that is associated with death. Further, the powers of darkness and the gods as well are associated with such destructiveness, and in fact, in tales such as "Without Benefit of Clergy," death is seen as the instrument of the gods. Suffering is not contemplated in terms of an individual, a particular class, or a race, but as a universal enemy that destroys civilization without any regard for the individual. If in *Phantom Rickshaw and Other Tales*, death is desired if only because it holds the promise associated with the unknown, in *Life's Handicap*, it becomes the instrument of unwarranted vengeance. Thus, all mankind is perceived as being trapped in the processes of life and death without being vouchsafed a knowledge of the Great Cause which controls these processes. If Jack, Jukes and Dravot were to some extent responsible for their tragic end, the same is perceived as being largely external to man. In fact, the subject matter of the tales is often so bleak, that it almost rivals the bitterness of Gloucester which makes him say: "As flies to wanton boys, are we to th' Gods / They kill us for their sport."[2] and in many of the tales, the gods inflict suffering "beyond the power of the pen" to express. Thus, in this collection the vision, as it emerges from the experience of the narrator and the characters, gets more complicated, for good and evil are no longer clearly separable. The God of Mercy and the God of Vengeance, life and death, mystery and reason all merge bewilderingly to become aspects of the one entity.

There are, however, tales that deal with a vision less terrifying, tales such as "The Incarnation of Krishna Mulvaney" where the experience of the characters is relatively more happy, and "Moti Guj--

Mutineer" which begins in harmony and, after a brief encounter with chaos, ends with the restoration of order. These tales, largely realistic sketches of Indian life, seem to have been included for a purpose which links them with the more serious tales. The instructions on the art of story-telling which Kipling's guru passes on to his disciple, seems directly responsible for the inclusion of these light-hearted tales in this selection. "Tell them first," advised the old man, "of those things thou hast seen and they have seen together. Thus their knowledge will piece out the imperfections" (p.xi).[3] In response to this, Kipling includes tales about "things" that are common to him and the reader, and establishes a bond between himself as the story-teller and his reader/audience. The reader is able to accept as truth the myriad-essence of human experience which the story-teller then goes on to reveal in accordance with the instructions of his guru. Once he has gained the confidence of his audience, he is advised to "tell them of what thou alone hast seen, then what thou hast heard" (p.xi). "The world," states Gobind, himself a renowned story-teller, "is full of tales to him who listens" (p.xi),[4] and the tales which deal with what the narrator/story-teller has himself experienced and with stories he has heard are interesting from the point of view of Kipling's vision. "Bubbling Well Road,"[5] together with "The City of Dreadful Night"[6] and "The Mark of the Beast"[7] form the tales which deal with the narrator's encounter with the mysterious unknown. Beyond these tales are the strange and elusive stories that the narrator has "heard" and "collected from all places, and all sorts of people" (p. xiii).[8] The most interesting of these tales are "The Wandering Jew,"[9] "Without Benefit of Clergy,"[10] "At the End of the Passage,"[11] and "The Dream of Duncan Parrenness."[12] If the reader "listens" carefully, he is vouchsafed knowledge of the vision that guides the narrator in *Life's Handicap*. The narrator clearly recognizes his role as a visionary in the long line of seer-prophets. Thus, he begins this collection with a dialogue between him and his guru, one which illuminates the revelatory nature of his task, and ends it with a prayer of thanksgiving that reveals his sensitive understanding of the essential mystery that is life. Since the characters of the tales are ordinary mortals, not blessed with the power of vision, they do not comprehend the nature of the cosmic dimension to life that seems to be so much in evidence in the East. Thus, his tales inevitably end in tragedy for the characters, but there is hope where there is a seer who prays:

Help me to need no aid from men
That I may help such men as need ![13]

II

"These things happened," states the narrator of his eerie experience, "when the jungle grass was tall" (p. 47).[14] The deliberate avoidance of chronological time emphasizes the mysterious nature of the encounter with the unknown in "Bubbling Well Road." His physical quest which takes him "five miles west of Chachuran" into the "plumed jungle grass, that turns over in silver when the wind blows" (p. 48), is paralleled by his psychological one.[15] Like Jukes, he is on a hunt, chasing wild boar because "the big boar of the sounder owned foot long tushes" (p. 48) and he wants to "produce the tushes in after years and say that I had ridden him down in fair chase" (p. 48).

Once he is inside the thick jungle, however, the narrator is faced with the dangerous unknown and, instead of being the predator, becomes a prey to forces that he cannot comprehend. The "road" has taken him out of the known sphere into the mysterious space occupied by the bubbling well and the "eerie unseen voice" (p. 49). The dark unknown seems also to be an externalization of the narrator's unacknowledged subconscious and thus another self. Unlike the echo, this self does not merely repeat the narrator's frenzied calls to his errant dog, but "chuckles"; and laughs "in a peculiarly offensive manner" (p. 49), or so the narrator imagines.

Predictably, the quest terminates when the narrator is faced with a mirror-reflection of his self in the waters of a well. The disturbing fact, however, is that in the mirror he does not see his familiar physical features, but "black things" in water "as black as pitch with black scum atop" (p. 49). Whether the "things" which the well faithfully mirrors back to the men peering into the abyss ("A well so deep I could scarcely see the water in it") are a reflection of the dark side of the narrator's own psyche, or an indication of the mysterious trap set by the Powers is never ascertained, primarily because he himself refuses to interpret the significant experience. Instead of answering the call from the unknown, which would have led to a revelation, the narrator seeks the safety of the rational, defined world which lies before the jungle. Thus, he frantically looks for the "paths" out of the patch of darkness. Mere escape from this terrifying unknown is not sufficient for him, and he is consumed with the desire to destroy the unknown by burning the patch. The attempt results in failure, for the unknown defies definition, but, according to the narrator, the failure is due to a mere physical circumstance--"the grass was too green"--that can be rectified. On a hot summer's day, when the grass is dry, he hopes to "clear the mystery" with a "file of old newspapers" and a "box of matches" (p. 51). But the mystery the well hides will never be deciphered, the grass will always be too green. In running away from the well, the narrator refuses the call to adventure, and thus knowledge of the truth is forever closed to him.

If the exact nature of the narrator's experience remains a mystery, the implications of the confrontation are clear. The physical, as well as the mental and psychological space occupied by the well is perceived as being demonic, that which lures the traveller to destruction. But that this demonic space also exists within the narrator is undeniable, for the well merely mirrors the face of the man who peers--in this case, the narrator.[16] If this tale is unsatisfactory because the adventure remains incomplete, the tale "The City of Dreadful Night" is more satisfying because the narrator accepts the call to adventure and is vouchsafed the promised vision.

Once again, the narrator is out on the "road," but this time it is a road that takes him into the city of "Dreadful Night." The restlessness which takes him into the jungle in "Bubbling Well Road" on a mysterious quest, now takes him into the realm of the forces of darkness. The city by night is perceived as being the personification of this ominous darkness, together with the "yelling jackals," "cicalas," and the "dense, wet heat." These forces of night beckon to the narrator to plunge into the land of darkness and the narrator responds to the call: "I set my walking stick on end in the middle of the garden, and waited to see how it would fall. It pointed directly down the moonlit road that leads to the City of Dreadful Night" (p. 52). Metaphorically as well as literally, his quest takes him into the land of the dead while still alive, and the danger which he faces is one of death--of being swallowed by the forces of darkness whose realm he is invading. The narrator is, however, aware of the danger, for not only is he physically awake, but is also awake to the similarity between the universal sleep of the city and universal death. Thus he notes the fact that "the jawless skulls and rough-butted shank bones" of the Moslem dead sleep together with the "corpses disposed on beds in fantastic attitudes" (p. 53), and if the "jaws" of the dead gleam like "mother-o'-pearl," it seems to him that those of the "sleeping corpses" look "silvery white and ashen grey" (p. 53).

Into this world of deathly sleep, the narrator enters and is immediately struck by the supremacy of the Dark Powers over the forces of life. At first, his journalistic mind prevents him from observing the life that animates the millions who form the very structure of the city, and all he sees is death, which robs the living of dignity, and this is what he catalogues: "'A leper asleep; and the remainder wearied coolies, servants, small shop-keepers, and drivers from the hack-stand hard by. The scene--a main approach to Lahore city, and the night a warm one in August'" (p. 53). But, he soon realizes that the nightmarish nature of the mysterious dark is not so easily dismissable. Instead of recording mere sensations, he makes an attempt to penetrate to the very essence of the powers that brood over the city at night. Thus, he is able to distinguish between "all that one could see" and "all that there was to be seen" (p. 53). It is interesting to note how different the scene appears to him now that he has shed his journalistic apparatus. He perceives that "the witchery of the moonlight" (which the journalist in him did not see) is responsible for transforming the city--ordinary enough in daylight--into the land of the dead at night. It is this witchery that threatens the world of the living in the form of the "rigid silver statue" which flanks the "long line of the naked dead" (p. 53), and illuminates only to expose "more corpses; more stretches of moonlit white road . . . and again more corpses" (p. 54).[17]

If death has claimed all these vast millions of people in sleep, the narrator seems to be questing for the forces of life which lie dormant beneath the mask of death. Thus, his search continues and the road takes him beyond the lines of the dead to the place of supreme affirmation--the Mosque of Wazir Khan. Stepping over "corpses," he reaches at last the sacred space of religion which battles against the Powers of Darkness. Significantly, the narrator chooses to "climb to the top of the great Minars, and thence to look down on the city" (p. 56), thus recreating the role of the protector--the muezzin who climbs the minars five times daily to remind the faithful of the power and supremacy of God over creation. But the narrator is not aware of the significance of the mosque, which stands defiantly in the midst of the very forces of darkness. Gazing at the sleeping millions from the vantage point provided by the soaring minarets, it appears to him as though he were watching a scene painted by one of the naturalists. The "pitiless moon" exposes "pit-like" courtyards and a chance cloud causes the "city and its inhabitants" to "fade into masses of black and deeper black" (p. 57).

Just as the narrator seems about to give in to overwhelming despair at the condition of mankind, the dark sky is rent with the muezzin's call "Allah Ho Akbar." "It is," states the narrator in this moment of revelation, "as though he were flinging his defiance to the far-off horizon where the summer lightning plays and leaps like a bared sword" (p. 58). If the powers of darkness are visualized in terms of the sinister, the power of God is understood as being equally forceful. Thus, the cosmic fight is well balanced; the "pitiless moon" is challenged by the "summer lightning." This moment forms the climax of the quest, for in accepting the power of religion and the sacred eternity of the mosque, the narrator reverts from hope to despair. Death, as he realizes, is not the final victor, but the necessary corollary to life.

Having been vouchsafed a revelation of the cosmic struggle, the narrator accepts his role as protector of the unaware, sleeping millions. Together with the muezzin--the only other individual awake with him--he serves the "heat tortured hive" of humanity arranged on the side of the powers of good, the sun and daylight. It is significant, therefore, that it is only in the early hours of the morning that the narrator allows his vigil to relax into an "uneasy doze" (p. 58), for there is an influx of the forces of good into the night air in the form of "a slight--a very slight coolness in the atmosphere" (pp. 58-59). Like the priest in "Bubbling Well Road," having guided the helpless and unconscious city to daylight, he is now ready to plunge back into the shelter of his own home. With the "first light of dawn," he makes his way "homeward" (p. 59). The "night-watch" is over with sunrise, but the night claims its victory, even as daylight does, for "something borne on men's shoulders comes by . . . a woman's corpse going down to the burning-ghat" (p. 59).

The resignation which the narrator exhibits on seeing the corpse is significant. It indicates a comprehension of the complex relationship of the two opposing forces of life and death. If the city is the city of prayer, daylight, life and the forces of good, it is also the opposite, and if it claims some victory in the form of death, it also gains victory in the form of birth, regeneration, of which the dawn of the new day is the perfect symbol. It follows naturally, therefore, that the theory of cause and effect--important in understanding the tragedy that afflicts the characters of *Phantom Rickshaw and Other Tales*--is, in the experience of these characters an inadequate explanation of the tragedy common to man, death. If man is not responsible for the cosmic harmony or disharmony, and cannot control the mysterious workings of nature, then neither is he responsible for the tragedy that is death, nor can he ever conquer it. He is, in fact, trapped in an irrevocable process of life and death in which he is nonetheless an important participant. Once the narrator accepts this fundamental "truth" he is able to accept the "city" by "night," and all it signifies, as well as by "day." While the man of imagination is able to comprehend and accept the harsh truth, the average "sleeping" man cannot and thus must remain unaware of the larger cosmic dimension to life or shrug it off as a nightmare. The narrator is aware of the necessity of preserving the "veil" for the vast majority of fallen mankind, as is made evident in his narration of Fleete's horrifying experience in "The Mark of the Beast".

The narrator begins the tale with a generalization: "East of the Suez, some hold that the direct control of providence ceases; Man being there handed over to the power of the Gods and Devils of Asia, and the Church of England Providence only exercising an occasional and modified supervision in the case of Englishmen" (p. 290). He goes on to add, "this theory accounts for some of the more unnecessary horrors of life in India; it may be stretched to explain my story" (p. 290). The terms he uses indicate his attitude to the concept of the "theory". While he is aware that theories are created by man in order to rationalize the incomprehensible, he sees the necessity for such theorising and uses theory in this story as a filter through which a complex vision becomes comprehensible to the common man, whom he is addressing.

The story itself is one of sacriligious pollution of the sacred space of a temple. Fleete, under the influence of alcohol is led to defiling the statue of Hanuman by "grinding the ash of his cigar-butt into the forehead of the red stone image" (p. 292). Applying his own Biblical knowledge, Fleete unknowingly reveals the enormity of the offence by equating his act with the very first homicide on earth--Cain's murder of Abel. Thus, he proudly informs his companions that he has made "The Mark of the B-beasht !" (p. 292) But, as Cain was branded with the knowledge of his offence, Fleete's action arouses the powers of Nemesis in the form of the loathsome "Silver Man" who emerges from a "recess behind the image of the God" (p. 293), himself an image of the deathly-cold power of Nemesis, to brand Fleete with a mark on the breast. Ironically, this "mark" develops into the mark of the "B-beasht", whereas the statue remains untouched, unpolluted. It is Fleete's self which is polluted as becomes evident in his degeneration into a beast. He begins to crawl on all fours, snarls like a "wolf," and relishes the taste of blood. Both the narrator and Strickland are horrified. "We were," realizes the narrator, "dealing with a beast that had once been Fleete" (p. 299). It is the death of a human being that the narrator records.

To create a human being out of a wild animal is not the task of a doctor, as both the narrator and Strickland realize. It is beyond any "doctor's work" (p. 300), and Dumoise's reaction merely confirms their belief. To Dumoise, the religious-psychological problem is merely "hydrophobia." So, it is not through the powers of science that Fleete is saved, but through Strickland, who has a partial understanding of the significance of the sequence of events. It is he who evolves a plan to trap the Silver Man without causing any further offence to the incensed Powers, a plan not revealed to the reader for it "cannot be put down here," states the narrator.

Both Strickland and the narrator are convinced that Fleete brought on the punishment by his own action. However, the question of responsibility is once again deliberately blurred by the eerie events which follow. Strickland, on going back to the temple to apologise for the defilement is told in no uncertain terms that "no white man had ever touched the idol and that he was an incarnation of all the virtues labouring under a delusion" (p. 305). Did the terrifying experience never take place ? Or, is this the Indian way of explaining that all is "maya"--illusion ? There are no answers. The whole experience baffles both the narrator and Strickland and it takes a few years before they find themselves capable of reviewing the incident "dispassionately" (p. 306). Even then, they do not have any explanations to offer. As the narrator admits, even revealing the experience to the "public" is not likely to "clear up the mystery" (p. 306). However, the reasons he provides are the wrong ones and they seem to have been deliberately provided. Therefore, what he leaves unsaid is more important than what he states. "In the first place," states the narrator, "no one will believe a rather unpleasant story, and in the second, it is well known to every right-minded man that the gods of the heathen are stone and brass, and any attempt to deal with them otherwise is justly condemned" (p. 306). But, it is exactly the last reason which, the narrator and every "right-minded man" knows may not be true.

Finally, if it is an illusion, as the priests say it is, then Fleete is not responsible for his actions from the beginning of the eerie experience to the end. In fact, he awakens after the struggle for his soul is over, unaware of the events of the last two days. Thus, the ending is left deliberately vague, for, the common man such as Fleete must be allowed to exist in relative ignorance of the larger cosmic dimension of life. It is left to the man of imagination, such as Strickland or the narrator, capable of grasping the notion of a larger force, to delve into this great unknown and grapple with experiences that defy analysis.

If the experiences which the narrator himself undergoes or witnesses are strange, eerie and involve a struggle with "unseen" forces (in "Bubbling Well Road" the owner of the mysterious voice is never seen; in "The City of Dreadful Night" the evil is not present in any concrete form, but seems to have invaded the earth) of which "night" and "death" seem to be the executors, the vision in tales which the narrator has ostensibly collected from other sources gets increasingly more grim. Death, in one form or another destroys millions, while fear or death drives others to agonizing encounters with the indomitable adversary..

III

The sky is lead and our faces are red,
And the gates of Hell are opened and riven
And the winds of Hell are loosened and driven,
And the dust flies up in the face of Heaven,
And the clouds come down in a fiery sheet,

Heavy to raise and hard to be borne.[18]

In an atmosphere that traps man, with all the elements seemingly against the powers of good, all that the weary race of man can do is surrender. Thus,

. . . the soul of man is turned from his meat,
Turned from the trifles for which he has striven
Sick in his body, and heavy-hearted,
And his soul flies up like the dust in the sheet
Breaks from his flesh and is gone and departed,
As the blasts they blow on the Cholera horn.[19]

Clearly, in the poem which forms the epigram to "At the End of the Passage," man is envisaged as being a bewildered creature caught in a metaphysical trap, and his physical degeneration closely parallels his mental and psychological disintegration. If cholera is the instrument of Death, "hag-ridden" nightmares and obsession with the self are the symbols of psychological surrender to the forces of darkness. Thus, it is the "shadow inside" John Hay, the protagonist of "The Wandering Jew," that grows "larger and blacker" and which speeds him on his journey towards the very death he has made it his life's goal to defeat. "His fear of death," as the narrator comments, "was driving him mad" (p. 11). The obsession with this invisible enemy takes him on a quest for personal, physical immortality. Out of the half-crazed depths of his mind arises a vision which (according to him), holds the secret of immortality. In order to gain immortality, therefore, he follows closely the knowledge revealed to him and this makes him into a modern day Wandering Jew accompanied by the belief that "who goes round the world easterly gains one day" (p. 11).

Thus, John Hay moves perpetually towards the rising sun. Even his journey never varies and never progresses, but is in itself a circular, entrapping movement. Not only is the route he takes fixed, but even the number of days it takes him to circle the globe is fixed. "Thirteen days in the train" from Calais to Calcutta whence he proceeds to America and returns to Calais from America "in twelve days over two months" (p. 12) having saved "four and twenty hours of precious time" (p. 12). While Hay believes that he is successful in his fight against time, his physical constitution betrays the effects of the irrevocable process of ageing. Time wasted in "watching the white wake spinning behind the sterm of the swiftest steamers, or the brown earth flashing past the windows of the fastest train" (p. 12) leaves him with "parched lips . . . shaking hands and . . . eyes that turned eternally to the East" (p. 13). Time has gained yet another victory, spelling out the absolute certainty of the decay which Hay believes he has conquered.

Furthermore, Time does not spare Hay the spiritual degradation which results from his naive attempt to fight the cosmic forces. It is with this pathetic figure of a broken man with broken dreams that the story ends. In an obscure seaside village in India, Hay submits to the madness which takes over when he realizes that his goal is unattainable. He submits to a "mad" scheme to hang from the roof by ropes and let the "round earth swing free beneath him" (p. 13) in the hope that by so doing he will be the equal of the "undying sun" (p. 13). But, even in his madness he is worried by fears that the noise he hears "without" is not the "thunder of the wheeling world" but merely the "noise of the surf" (p. 14) and no one answers his question: "Why does not the sun always remain over my head ?" (p. 14) Ironically enough, it is by the side of the ever-renewing forces of nature--the sun and the sea--that he plays out his tragic farce to the bitter end. He becomes an immovable legend surrounded by the flux of time and hence an anachronism. "Men say" states the narrator, "that if you wander along the southern coast of India, you shall find in a neatly whitewashed little bungalow, sitting in a chair swung from the roof . . . an old man who forever faces the rising sun, a stop watch in his hand, racing against eternity" (p. 14).

The quest for physical immortality which mocks the individual in his attempt to escape the trap of death, tortures Duncan Parrenness in the form of a revelatory dream in the tale "The Dream of Duncan Parrenness". The dream is brought on by Duncan's random recollections of the death of "those young bloods that came eastward with me in the same ship" (p. 77) and the insensitive joy at his own escape from a similar fate. Combined with this, the unbidden recollection of his less than exemplary life troubles him with the belief that supreme justice may demand his "lease on life" as retribution. The recollections terminate in a challenge flung at "Heaven and Earth" that "I, Duncan Parrenness was a writer in the service of the company and afraid of no man" (p. 78). The retribution, however, is not to come from the impassive "Moon" or "Great Bear" but from his own unconscious in the form of a dream. It is not Death that demands a price, but the diseased self that he sees sitting at the end of his bed. "I saw that his face was my very own" states Duncan, "but marked and lined and scarred with the furrows of disease and much evil living--as I once, when I was (Lord help me) very drunk indeed, having seen mine own face all white and drawn and grown old, in a mirror" (p. 80). The "black things" reflected back to the narrator in "Bubbling Well Road" are the things which now confront the dreaming Duncan.

In the horrifying barter that follows, Duncan is divested of three qualities associated with the powers of good and life-giving forces. The first quality "Myself" demands is his "trust in man." But since it soon becomes apparent that he has already lost his trust in mankind, Myself's demand merely seals the loss. The next quality the shadow takes from him is his "faith in women" (p. 81), once again, something he has already lost. Finally, he is divested of "as much as remained to me of my boy's soul and conscience" (p. 81). This last loss leaves behind a "deadly coldness at the heart" (p. 82). Duncan attempts to rationalize the loss of all his human qualities by explaining it in terms of a necessary movement from innocence to experience, the exchange having left "all the boy . . . burnt and scarred away," so that he passes "all at one step to the more sorrowful state of manhood" (p. 82). What "manhood" reveals to him is the knowledge that he has "the strength to live as long as God or the Devil pleases" (p. 82). Instead of getting the desired unlimited freedom from fear of death, he is doomed to a death-in-life existence, devoid of the human qualities of love, faith, and goodness, that come of possessing a conscience. As a substitute for these qualities, he is offered a gift by Myself, a "little piece of dry bread" (p. 82) The mocking gesture echoes a similar gesture by Time in the face of John Hay, and, in fact both are aware of the presence of an inimical, superior force.

Mere knowledge of the existence of the superior force, however, does not assure success in the battle against the adversary. Thus, though Hay makes an attempt to fight his adversary, Time, he does not succeed. Similarly Duncan, who watches his ego battle against itself in the form of a shadow, loses the fight even before it begins. If Hay loses because his limited human nature prevents him from understanding the real nature of Time, Duncan loses because he has mis-understood the nature of life. In his desire to gain a "lease on life" he forgets that it is a piece of "dry bread" without the positive qualities of faith, love and trust.

The battle can only be won if the characters make an attempt to quest for the meaning behind the manifestations of the superior powers, as the narrator does in "The City of Dreadful Night." But, limited comprehension results in a tragic and futile attempt to assert the self through the search for immortality. The tale which best exemplifies the tragedy which afflicts the common man in an utterly incomprehensible manner is "Without Benefit of Clergy." In this story, semi-comprehension of the truth dawns on Holden only after he has drained the "Bitter Waters" to the dregs. It is with a stanza from the poem that the tale begins.

> Before my Spring I garnered Autumn's gain,
> Out of her time my field was white with grain,
> The year gave up her secrets to my woe,
> Forced and deflowered each sick season lay,
> In mystery of increase and decay;
> I saw the sunset 'ere men saw the day,
> Who am too wise in that I should not know.
>
> (p. 212)

Holden's and Ameera's experience is almost a continuation of that of Trejago and Bisesa in "Beyond the Pale" except that, in this tale the relationship is more enduring. However, though their love seems to be stable, there is a general atmosphere of fear which infects and soon defines their relationship. Their love has its origins in a contract and remains one till Ameera's death breaks it. The relationship never develops into the sacred bonds of matrimony. Thus Ameera regards herself as a slave until she becomes the mother of his child. Even then, the child is seen as a bond, "for the love of a man, and particularly a white man" is, according to Ameera, "an inconstant affair," but it might be "held fast by a baby's hand" (p. 214). Fear at the tenuousness of their relationship is abetted by the deception involved. To the world, Holden is a "bachelor," a "free man" (p. 214), and his bachelor's residence is separate from the house he regards as "home." The latter is an isolated paradise, and when "the big wooden gate was bolted behind him," Holden imagines himself "King in his own territory, with Ameera for Queen" (p. 214).

This double life, which naturally enough requires double standards, works its way into the relationship and culminates in the application of the standards of one to the other. Thus, to Holden, Ameera and her mother appear of a lower order than his son. His parting gesture--when he comes to see his son for the first time--reduces them to the level of the Anglo-Indian "ayah"[20] as Holden thrusts some money into Ameera's mother's hands saying, "See that my baba gets fat and finds all that he needs" (p. 218). Ameera reacts instinctively to the insult. "I am his mother," she retorts, "and no hireling. Shall I look to him more or less for the sake of money ? Mother, give it back. I have borne my lord a son" (p. 218).

All the doubts and fears are forgotten, however, in the meeting of the two individuals from East and West. According to the narrator, "those were months of absolute happiness to Holden and Ameera--happiness withdrawn from the world, shut in behind the wooden gate that Pir Khan guarded" (p. 225). It is just such an attempt on Frederick Henry's and Catherine's part--in Hemingway's *A Farewell to Arms*--to build an isolated heaven while the rest of the world suffers the death-pangs of war, that causes Nemesis to destroy their paradise. It is a similar desire, which the narrator regards as an irresponsible one, that breaks so systematically the world that these two have made for themselves. Tragedy strikes suddenly and in its most dreaded form--death. The narrator rationalizes the cause of the tragedy--Tota's death--by theorising: "the delight of that life was too perfect to endure. Therefore it was taken away as many things are taken away in India--suddenly and without warning" (p. 227). Yet, there is no answer to the question "Why ?," even the narrator's surmises seem to be part of a theory that may be "stretched" to account for the unaccountable.

Meanwhile, in the world surrounding their own secluded heaven strengthened by the death of their son, the "powers" are busy preparing vengeance, for "they had allowed thirty million people four years of plenty wherein men had fed well and the crops were certain and the birth-rate rose year by year" (p. 231). It is the "blood-red dhak-tree" that flowers early as a "sign of what was coming" (p. 231) and it indicates the nature of the tragedy about to inflict itself on the land. "Nature," as the Deputy Commissioner reflects, "is going to audit her accounts with a big red pencil" (p. 232). Death devastates the subcontinent, disaster that no one understands but everyone merely records as does the narrator:

> On the heels of the spring-reapings came a cry for bread . . . then came the cholera . . . it struck a pilgrim gathering of half a million at a sacred shrine. Many died at the feet of their god . . . it smote a walled city and killed two hundred a day . . . they died by the roadside . . . and the earth turned to iron lest man should escape death by hiding in her (p. 236).

No one questions the cause of the tragedy. Even the narrator is reduced to theorising: "It was a red and heavy audit, for the land was very sick and needed a little breathing space 'ere the torrent of cheap life should flood it anew" (p. 235). Soon, "gaps" are filled and the process continues, "because it is so ordained" (p. 236) by the ubiquitous powers.

In the world torn by universal catastrophe, it is impossible for Holden and Ameera to survive in an isolated paradise. Holden seems to be aware of this, and is "absolutely certain that her (Ameera's) death would be demanded" (p. 236), so that when the call comes, he "laughed aloud" (p. 236) and in common with thousands of others, Ameera succumbs to the "black Cholera" (p. 236). The tragedy in one small household is seen in perspective, as one amongst thousands of households suffering the same agony. In fact, Ameera's death loses much of its impact in front of the welcome "end" of the "audit," which means the triumph of the forces of life over death. She dies listening to the first few drops of rain that herald the end of the period of torment. Only, she and thousands of others have had to be sacrificed in order to ensure the continuation of the cycle of regenerative life and thus, on one level, the personal tragedy becomes a universal one.

Whether Holden plays the game of love, or the four characters of "At the End of the Passage" play "whist" in defiance of the supreme powers, they emerge the losers, for all seek "life, liberty and . . happiness" not within themselves, but in external objects. Thus, Mottram, Lowndes and Spurtow, three of the four players in the story envy Hummeil, their host, for "he has an actual roof . . . over his head. He sees one train daily. He can get beer and sodawater and ice 'em when God is good" (p. 246). Yet, it is for this physically well provided man that the "gates of hell are opened and riven" (p. 246). While a dust-storm rages without, Hummeil reveals the queer torment that makes him much less lucky than his companions imagine him to be. For Hummeil, life has lost its value and he is beyond rationalising existence, through religion or love. It is an illusion, according to him, to believe that "sacred thoughts" counteract the evil within and without the self. Having dispelled all illusions, including the illusion that God and man enjoy a harmonious relationship ("It is," he states, "an insult to the intelligence of the Deity to pretend we're anything but tortured rebels") he is faced by a terrifying void which only death can terminate, or so he believes.

Unfortunately, death which does not mean the annihilation of the senses, poses an equally grave threat to him. His plea to the world of science is literally to "let me sleep," for "it isn't enough merely to let me dream" (p. 255). The black void, the "place" which haunts him is partially revealed in the "broken whispers" with which he communicates his agony and terror to another. It is a "blind face" that "chases him down corridors," a "blind face that cries and cannot wipe its eyes" (p. 259). Even the world of dreams is turned into a perpetual nightmare, to prevent which he submits to another sort of torture--that of intense physical pain, by rowelling himself with a "spur." He is caught, then, in a vicious trap. The world of sleep, of rest, is denied him because it is nightmare ridden. At the same time, the world of waking existence is a torture without its necessary counterpart, sleep. The only way out seems to be through death. The trap closes in on the tormented man and ends predictably in death. If while living, death seems to offer the only release, in death it seems as though Hummeil touches the very nadir of horror, for death leaves behind its peculiar stamp in his "eyes" for the living to witness. It is "in the staring eyes" that is "written terror beyond the expression of any pen" (p. 262).

The power of death lies beyond the understanding of science, and Spurstow the doctor is unable to determine the cause of the death. "As far as I can make out," he states, "he died from--oh, anything; stoppage of the heart's action, heat-apoplexy or some other visitation" (p. 263). Lowndes is closer to the truth when he states: "He was scared to death. Look at those eyes" (p. 263). It is the servant who instinctively touches on the mystery, for he believes that "this that was my master has descended into the Dark Places, and there has been caught because he was not able to escape with sufficient speed. We have the spur for evidence that he fought with fear" (p. 263). Still, the definite cause remains a mystery, and, if Spurstow discovers the reason behind the "thing" in Hummeil's eyes, he does not reveal it, though he emerges "very white" from a confrontation with the "thing." It is with the sense of unresolved mystery--not only of death, but of life as well--that the narrator ends the tale: "There may be Heaven--there must be Hell / Meantime, there is our life here, we-ell ?" (p. 266)

The vision which emerges from the experience of the characters and the narrator is extremely bleak, and this gloom is symbolised in the atmosphere of the tales. It is no mere coincidence that so many of them are set in the Hot Season, which, instead of being merely a part of a natural cycle, assumes demonic proportions as the instrument of inimical forces, unseen and fearful. The gates of hell open not only for Hummeil, but for masses of pilgrims, Tota, Ameera and countless others. The rationalization offered is that "East of the Suez is a universe incomprehensible to man." If the vision is so bleak, the hope of redemption seems to recede. Yet the poem with which the collection ends, "L'envoi," holds the promise of future redemption. If the "Great overseer" is frightening, he is also the origin of good.

The ability to comprehend the seemingly paradoxical aspects of the one and the same "Overseer" is necessary to an understanding of the essence of life and death, or so the narrator--who seems to be identical with Kipling the story-teller--appears to believe. If the God of Mercy and Love is to exist, so must his contrary, the God of Divine Wrath and Vengeance, both aspects of the one being. Thus, the story-teller begins and ends the collection with a vision of an Edenic world and the possibility of grace that acts as a corrective to the tormented universe in which one is unable to see beyond the threat of death.

IV

The Preface itself is a vision of all the harmonious forces that are responsible for the creation of an Eden on earth and an extension of the goodness of the "Great Overseer" to whom the story-teller offers thanksgiving at the end of the collection. The setting is the sacred space of the "Chubara" where peace and love reign supreme, where "clumps of mangoes sprouted from between the bricks; great pipal trees overhung the well-windlass that whined all day; and hosts of parrots tore through the trees. Crows and squirrels were tame in that place, for they knew that never a priest would touch them" (p. viii). But, most important of all, the monastery is the "place of call and rest" for thousands of "wanderers" on their journey through life. "Mahomedan, Sikh and Hindu mixed equally under the trees" (p. vii) and for old men such as Gobind, it is a place to await death as the welcome end to a long and fulfilled life. In fact, Gobind has learnt to master Time, and appears almost to control his own death. It is from such a "guru"[21] that the narrator learns his knowledge of the essential unity of opposites.

Between Gobind and the narrator is established the bond of story-tellers, and the former teaches his disciple the immense value of story-telling, which lies in its creation of communitas. "I told many tales" he says, "and heard many more at the rest-houses in the evening when we were merry at the end of the march" (p. ix). The story-teller is also committed to revealing the truth, and it is through his tales that he does so. Thus Gobind instructs the narrator about the essential "truth" that lies in fiction (fiction--as Kipling states elsewhere, is Truth's "elder sister") so that "a tale that is told is a true tale as long as the telling lasts" (p. x). It is about the essential truths that the narrator wishes to write, about "life and death, men and women and Love and Fate" (p. ix). The truth is hard for man to accept and if life is truth, so is death. Yet, if the narrator in his honesty sees the overwhelming power of death over man, he also sees its absolute insignificance in front of a sage like Gobind--a prime symbol of the immense power of good.

The selection ends with a hymn of thanksgiving which celebrates the mighty power and justice of God the Father, or Shiva the destroyer in Hindu myth, as well as the immense love and mercy of God the Son, Christ, or Vishnu the preserver, and the imagination of God the Holy Spirit or Brahma the creator, responsible for giving the supreme gift of life to man. The "Great Overseer" is addressed as "Master," who lives removed from man "In that dread Temple of Thy Worth;" as well as the merciful one who knows "The depth and dream of my desire, / The bitter paths wherein I stray;" as well as the God of divine Imagination, who, "lest all thought of Eden fade, / Bring'st Eden to the craftsman's brain, / Godlike to muse o'er his own trade / And Manlike stand with God again."[22]

It is this vision of the essential unity of contraries that the seer/ story-teller achieves, and his greatest fear is that this knowledge will be taken from him. His only prayer is to be allowed to retain the vision: "Take not that vision from my ken; / Oh whatsoe'er my spoil or speed." The prayer, however, does not stem from the selfish desire to attain personal salvation, but from the desire to reveal his knowledge for the good of mankind:

> Help me to need no aid from men
> That I may help such men as need ![23]

NOTES

1. Most critics have noted the importance of death in Kipling's tales. Shamsul Islam in *Kipling's 'Law': A Study of His Philosophy of Life* (London: Macmillan, 1975) states that "One is always conscious of the presence of death in Kipling's Indian stories" (p. 64). Noel Annan, in "Kipling's Place in the History of Ideas," reprinted in *Kipling's Mind and Art*, ed. Andrew Rutherford (London: Oliver and Boyd, 1965) states: "The picture of India which Kipling painted in his first four volumes of short-stories . . . is that of a society which politically, nervously, physically and spiritually, quivered on the edge of a precipice. . . . Here Nature was inconceivably hostile. . . . Death always at a man's elbow" (p. 102).

2. William Shakespeare, *King Lear* (Boston: Houghton Mifflin, 1974), IV, i, 36-37.

3. Preface to *Life's Handicap* (*L.H.*), p.xi. All references to the tales in this collection are to the Macmillan edition of 1896.

4. Ibid., p.xi.

5. "Bubbling Well Road" in *L.H.* The tale was first published in the *Civil and Military Gazette* on 18 Jan., 1888.

6. "The City of Dreadful Night" in *L.H.* The tale was first published in the *Civil and Military Gazette*, 10 Sept., 1885.

7. "The Mark of the Beast" in *L.H.* The tale was first published

in *Pioneer*, 12 July, 1890.

8. Preface to *L.H.* , p. xiii.

9. "The Wandering Jew" in *L.H.* The tale was first published in the *Civil and Military Gazette*, 14 April, 1889.

10. "Without Benefit of Clergy" in *L.H.* The tale was first published in this collection.

11. "At the End of the Passage" in *L.H.* The tale was first published in this collection.

12. "The Dream of Duncan Parrenness" in *L.H.* The tale was first published in the *Civil and Military Gazette*, 25 Dec., 1884.

13. "L'envoi," the poem with which the collection ends.

14. "Bubbling Well Road" in *L.H.*, p. 47.

15. In Mythology, the quest of the hero almost always takes him into the unknown, and is therefore dangerous. Joseph Campbell in *The Hero With a Thousand Faces* (Princeton: U. Press, 1968) in his first chapter "The Call to Adventure" states that the refusal of the call to adventure results in a stunted personality.

16. There is an interesting parallel with Alice's adventures in *Through the Looking Glass*. Alice too sees a reflection of herself in a mirror that distorts. This does not deter her, and she accepts the call to adventure, and emerges a Queen, a fully developed individual.

17. There is a tradition in Literature which associates "sleep" with death, as the former means the act of rendering up of the senses which becomes permanent in death. Thus, in Shakespeare the idea of "death counterfeiting sleep" is an important one.

18. From the poem which forms the epigraph to "At the End of the Passage."

19. Ibid., p. 241.

20. An Indian term applied to a maid servant whose main task is to look after the children.

21. The relationship between the guru and his disciple is considered sacred in India. In fact, the guru could be considered the equivalent of the "good genius" which is supposed to inspire poets. Thus, it is fitting that Kipling should invoke the spirit of his guru to reveal to the reader his own belief in the power of the Imagination, especially as it manifests itself in the Word.

22. "L'envoi."

23. Ibid.

The Role of Love, Imagination and the Law in Kipling's Vision

I

A much discerning public hold
The singer generally sings
Of personal and private things
And prints and sells his past for gold.

Whatever I may here disclaim
The very clever folk I sing to
Will most indubitably cling to
Their pet delusion just the same.[1]

So sings a disillusioned poet, but as the rest of the poem makes clear, he admits to a great responsibility towards this very unappreciative audience--that of revealing his vision to them as his Greek ancestors did, singing to man of the mysterious truths of his tribe. If part of the truth is to be found in what Roskies terms "The God of Things as They Are,"[2] the analysis of the modern condition of chaos also reveals the truth about "freedom and the limits of freedom."[3] If too, Death is recognized as limiting man's corporeal existence, a higher truth supersedes the despair at the knowledge of the inevitable physical disintegration of the cosmos. Thus, it is not surprising that bards are traditionally represented as being blind, for it is the truth of the Imagination that they see and reveal. This higher truth lies in the knowledge of the supremacy of the Imagination, the link between eternal order (the "Great Overseer" of "L'envoi") and man.

Though the experience of the characters in the tales discussed in the last three chapters attests to the rampant existence of chaos and the dark forces, they must be seen in perspective--as stories that form part of the memory of the narrator, whose imagination is responsible ultimately for creating them, and through them a semblance of the divine order. This he does by imposing on the various experiences the form and structure of verbal expression, i.e., by employing the techniques of oral narration. The creativity of the story-teller is thus a tribute to the "Great Overseer" who first created--through the power of his imagination--order in the form of life out of the void that was chaos. Thus, part of Kipling's vision is a celebration of creation by divine imagination of the Holy Ghost or Brahma.[4]

Through exercising his creative faculties for the benefit of mankind, the narrator-seer surrenders his ego to an altruistic concern for his race. The archetypal figure of the poet is therefore Christ-Vishnu. It is this aspect of self-sacrificial love that is revealed in "The Children of the Zodiac," "Cold Iron," and *Kim*

Finally, the poet-seer reveals a knowledge of the "Law," of the God of Wrath, in himself personifying the God of Love, while imitating the God of Imagination by creating in the vein of divine creation. It is "law" that enables man to be true to himself, allows for an individuality based on its contrary--the social fabric. The tales "How Fear Came" and "The Spring Running" from the *Jungle Book* deal most clearly with this "law" that is the way to a higher freedom. While most critics are agreed on the fact that it is the "law" as enumerated in the *Jungle Book* that offers the solution to chaos, they seem unaware of the importance of the imagination and love as concepts in Kipling's vision. Thus, his vision cannot be analysed merely in terms of the *Jungle Book* or the "law" but in terms of the whole body of his work.

II

What boots it on the Gods to call ?
Since, answered or unheard,
We perish with the Gods and all
Things made--except the Word.

Yet they, who use the Word assigned
To hearten and make whole,
Not less than Gods have served mankind
Though vultures rend their soul.[5]

The first and last stanzas of "A Recantation" are really an adequate defence of the story-teller and his task--to make "whole" the fragmented chaos that is part of modern man. It is interesting to note that of all creation, in Biblical history, it is in the form of the "Word" that life as it is conceived of in human terms, was first created. In the Gospel of St. John, chapter I.i, is stated: "In the beginning was the Word and the Word was with God and the Word was God."[6] Thus, the "Word" is at once synonymous with Divinity and a part of it which devolved into creation. It is the story-teller's respect for the divine "Word" that is being celebrated in this poem, and if he must give in to personal death, it is suggested that his use of language to "hearten and make whole" will make him immortal, a god.

It was the ancient bard's ability to recreate in words the awesome, mythic origins of man that brought him the respect and privilege of being the link between the tribe of man and the otherwise unavailable divine presence. Thus, Homer, Virgil, Dante and Milton appealed to the divine Muse to inspire them with the "Word" so that they could reveal the truth to man.[7] So too, Kipling believed he had a "Daemon"[8] who inspired him with his vision. It is interesting to note that the vision of the great bards, in common with Kipling's, records the terror of the unknown, more specifically, death. If Odysseus or Ulysses as he is called in *The Aeneid*, visits the forbidden land of the dead, Dante has to go to Inferno before he can reach Paradise, and Milton plunges into the tormented hell of Satan and his followers guarded by Death and Sin, before proceeding to sing of the glories of the heavenly kingdom.

In singing of a past common to man, the bard or story-teller hopes to recreate the communality, harmony and wholeness that existed before the Fall, with a difference--that he hopes to create paradise on earth and is not merely regressing into an unavailable past. Story-telling or legend creating in secular time seems to have a similar aim in mind--to combat the increasing solipsism of man and his fear of the unknown by creating the bond of communitas, and it is the "Word" that is used as the medium of communication. Oral narration, therefore, helped create a sense of community and a sense of being part of the mythic process of which the Bard sang, while being irrevocably a part of the temporal universe. In Kipling's tales, oral narration is used in an attempt to recapture something of this communality and awareness of the presence of divinity. A number of his tales begin with statements which make them seem legendary. "Thousands of years ago" begins "The Children of the Zodiac,"[9] "this was how it happened; and the truth is also an allegory of Empire" begins "Naboth."[10] Other tales refer to stories that have already appeared to create the illusion of a continuous legend such as the ancient Indian folktales, the *Panchatantra*. However, what links Kipling's tales irrevocably with the epics in the oral tradition is his subject matter. His concern is with the chaotic human condition which finds symbolic expression in the sphynx-like mystery that surrounds death. By creating a legend of man's struggle with life, and his overcoming of it to achieve divinity, as with Buddha, Christ and Odysseus, the story-teller hopes to infuse a similar spirit of divinity into his audience. "It is," as Leo the Man-God in "The Children of the Zodiac" states, "the only song I am allowed to sing. You must not be afraid of the Houses, even when they kill you" (p. 422).

There is, however, something which makes Kipling the story-teller and narrator quite distinctively a modern seer as opposed to the ancient Homeric Bard. Whereas earlier the bard's sacred position in the tribe was restricted only to himself and differentiated him from the rest of the tribe, in Kipling's tales, the emphasis is clearly not merely on communicating his vision to fallen man, but on creating a community of story-tellers. Thus, the whole world, which is "full of tales to him who listens,"[11] according to Gobind, becomes at once a community of tellers and listeners. In the Preface to *Life's Handicap*, therefore, Kipling deliberately includes all of mankind in his imagination. "These tales," he states, "have been collected from all places, and all sorts of people, from priests in the Chubara, from Ala Yar the carver, Jiwan Singh the carpenter, nameless men on steamers" and the list goes on.[12] The very technique, therefore, that Kipling uses in his short stories is a significant indication of the importance of the imagination in his vision which allows him to see "naught common on Thy earth."[13]

III

> Then a voice cried 'what shall come to the boy if thou art dead' and I was shaken back and forth in my self with pity for thee; and I said: 'I will return to my chela lest he miss the Way.' Upon this

> my soul . . . withdrew itself from the Great Soul with strivings and yearnings and retchings and agonies not to be told . . . I pushed world upon world for thy sake.[14]

The narrator-seer in his concern for mankind loses his egoist concern for his self and this achievement of the Keatsian negative capability forms part of Kipling's vision. According to Gilbert, it is the "movement of the artist from painful, self-centred contemplation of life to an almost Eastern surrender of the Self, a yielding of the personality to superior external forces" that lies at the "heart of the author's esthetic theory."[15] Certainly, it is for this loss of selfhood that the narrator appeals in "L'envoi," in the last two lines of the poem: "Help me to need no aid from men / That I may help such men as need !"[16] It is clearly on the lines of such a theory that "The Children of the Zodiac" published in 1891, and "Cold Iron" in 1910 are modelled.

So long as the children of the zodiac--the Ram, the Bull, the Lion, the Twins and the Girl--remain Gods, separate from the destinies of men, they are removed from the process of death and even from knowledge of the human condition. Thus, while they "listened" to the sorrows of mankind, they "could not understand" (p. 400) tears nor the laughter of joy, and wonder why "People shouted 'Ha ! Ha ! Ha !' for no cause" (p. 401). It is from mortals that these Gods learn to laugh and love, but they remain unaware of the implications of mortality and thus Leo in his innocence goes to the House of Scorpion to request that the race of man be allowed to live as "I--we do" (p. 404). Though Scorpion replies: "Your wish was granted long ago" (p. 404), irony lies in the fact that it is the gods who are to live like men and not vice versa. Leo the Poet's rite of passage begins immediately after his interview with the Scorpion,[17] at the end of which he learns to accept the doctrine of self-sacrifice.

The first step of his journey towards knowledge brings Leo face to face with his erstwhile companions in divinity, now mere servile animals, or so it seems to the naive poet. The Bull who blazed in the Empyrean is now willingly "yoked to a countryman's plough" (p. 408), even though it means being "goaded . . . till his flanks were red" (p. 405). To Leo's outraged response: "Gore that insolent to death" (p. 405), the Bull merely replies: "I cannot, the Scorpion has told me that someday . . . he will sting me where my neck is set on my shoulders, and that I shall die bellowing" (p. 405). Before death claims him, the Bull intends to serve the countryman to the best of his ability. A "scornful" Leo leaves the Bull only to find the "Ram" engaged in a similar service to mankind. The "new trouble" that has changed his "brethren" is incomprehensible to Leo, till Cancer the Crab assures him that the same fate is reserved for him too. "When the full moon fails to call the tide," warns the Crab, "I shall come for the one. When the other has taken the earth by the shoulders, I shall take the other by the throat" (pp. 408-09). Together with his death, the Crab predicts the nature of his service on earth; he shall take "the earth by the shoulders" through the power of his "throat." Leo, however, is as yet unaware of the importance of his role on earth, as despair at the knowledge that he and the Girl must die overtakes him. Back on earth, mortality and humanity clothe the two, so that it is "only" as a "man and a woman" (p. 410) that they face their former followers, sitting "hand in hand on the altar steps" in front of the shrine they had once graced. If Adam and Eve leave Paradise in Milton's *Paradise Lost* "hand in hand" to learn the lesson of the fortunate fall, it is with "white" and "frightened" faces that Leo and the Girl begin their lives as human beings.

The fear of death prevents Leo from living life as his brethren do. On the other hand, the aimless, eternal calm with which he passed thousands of human years does not seem possible either. "Driven forward by the fear of death" (p. 412), Leo approaches the Bull, for the latter seems to have found meaning in his fall. It is at the moment when the Bull requests him to "Sing . . . sing one of the songs that we sang when we thought we were all gods together" (p. 413), that Leo discovers the power to combat the fear of death. If he cannot "pull a plough" (p. 413), as the Bull scorns, he can "sing." Death recedes as he sings of "facts that he had not particularly noticed before the interview" (p. 414) with the Crab. He discovers knowledge and powers of perception he never knew he possessed. Because of his songs, the Bull ploughs "half a field more" than he should have done. From this moment onwards, Leo does not regret the loss of immortality, as the task of serving the race of man becomes meaningful to him.

However, Leo realizes the exacting nature of self-sacrifice only in the face of personal disaster, when death carries away his companion, the Girl. His first experience of sorrow makes Leo spiritually immortal though he does not realize it. At the moment when he suffers, he becomes one with the race of mankind through history--since man has known suffering from the moment of the fall--and also with contemporary man, whose suffering he has been unable to fully comprehend 'til this moment. All of mankind, even the other singers in competition with him, now appear to him as his brothers. In his altruistic concern for his audience, Leo drowns his personal sorrow, and it is precisely because he has "known all the sorrow that a man could know, including the full knowledge of his fall who had once been a god" (p. 419), that he can change his song from "one of sorrow to one of joy" (p. 419) at the request of his audience. It is in his songs that Virgo the Girl continues to live, so that "some of the women who remembered the Girl said: 'Surely that is the voice of Virgo. Only she could know so much about ourselves' " (p. 421). To them, Leo and Virgo are one.

Singing in defiance of death and personal tragedy, as Virgo had said he must, Leo is made aware of his contribution to mankind through his use of the "Word." A man who formed part of his audience, about to die, extends his gratitude to the poet, for "I should have run away," he admits, "but for your songs. My work is done, and I die without making a show of my fear" (p. 422). At this moment, Leo perceives that the prophecy of the Crab has come true, he has "taken the world by the shoulders." For Leo his work has just begun, but according to the prophecy, it is also the end, and death robs him of his divine gift, as the Crab grips his "throat." Death, fear of which had earlier prevented him from living, is now perceived as being his adversary primarily because it has the power to rob him of his ability to serve mankind. It is on this basis that Leo pleads with Death. "Let me be sure that my songs--" (p. 423) he begins, and Death completes the statement: "Make men brave ?" Though Leo must accept his fate in common with the rest of mankind, he dies unafraid and secure in the knowledge that like his fellow gods, he has served by using the "word" to "hearten and make whole" ("A Recantation") the race of fallen men.

Similarly, Gobind a seer-story-teller, dies unafraid for he has served mankind in his own way--reacquainted them with the truth that "the Gods walk on earth as they did, only man has not the faith to see."[18] The term of his life accomplished, he is ready to surrender to the inevitable. "Cold Iron" too has a similar vision to offer, as the human boy removed from the processes of mortality by supernatural powers is returned to a knowledge of mortality and the suffering of mankind through the power of "cold iron." On touching the symbol of humanity, The Boy is clamped within a ring of iron, making him a slave. Yet, according to Puck, the narrator of the tale, The Boy could have refused the change. Instead, he locks the ring around his neck himself, welcoming his role as servant of humanity. Bodelsen too sees a similar pattern in both the tales discussed above. According to him, in both tales, "the poet sacrifices himself in order to help mankind, losing his superhuman status in doing so."[19] However, he stops short of stating that the whole concept of divinity is being challenged, for the children of the zodiac and The Boy achieve true immortality through their very humanity, as the epigram to "The Children of the Zodiac" makes clear: "When half Gods go / The Gods arrive" (p. 401).

It is in *Kim* that this principle is clearly endorsed in the central figure, the Lama. The search for the elusive "River of the Arrow"[20] takes him through the path of renunciation to the supreme knowledge of the power of love. As Annan states, he finds "enlightenment and freedom--the comprehension of the order of things--through love."[21] Thus he rejects the isolated paradise which was his when he "reached the Great Soul" and meditated on the "Causes of all Things" for a "thousand years" (p. 472) for his "chela." It is only when he decides after great "strivings and yearnings and yearnings and retchings and agonies not to be told" (p. 472) to return, that he is vouchsafed a vision of the River of the Arrow. His quest culminates therefore, in a vision of service--to his chela, and he returns as he says "from the Threshold of Freedom to free thee from all sin" (p. 474).

It is the loss of selfhood that makes the poet in all these characters more receptive to the vision of which they sing till death claims them. If the Crab enlightens Leo, Cold Iron awakens knowledge in The Boy, as does the Great Soul in the Lama. However, the knowledge they gain as a result of their moment of illumination is, as Gilbert recognizes, "a menace to society." It is a threat to the "complacent society which does not appreciate how perfect and how reckless is the artist's commitment to reality."[22] It is because of his desire to restore the Edenic reality which existed before the fall,[23] that the poet feels it incumbent upon himself to sing of the way it can be done. Thus, the Lama sings of love, as does Leo and Baloo--the ancient bard of the jungle--as well. Baloo also sings of the "Law" which stands, as Angus Wilson suggests, as a "barrier" between "man and anarchy, and more importantly, between man and the probably meaningless death and destruction that awaits him and all his works."[24]

IV

> The Law of the Jungle--which is by far the oldest law in the world--has arranged for almost every kind of accident that may befall the Jungle people, till now its code is as perfect as time and custom can make it.[25]

Baloo, the old seer of the Jungle, teaches Mowgli the meaning and importance of this very Jungle Law which "no one could escape" as, in his words, "The Law was like the Giant Creeper, because it dropped across everyone's back" (p. 77). Though the Law seems to impose unnecessary restrictions to the impatient boy, in the tale "How Fear Came," he is made to see the necessity of obeying the Jungle Law if the Jungle is to survive the catastrophes Time metes out. The tale opens with the threat of death in the form of the drought. Hunger and thirst threaten to evolve into the extinction of the animals. When the Waingunga, a tributary of the sacred Ganges river, dries to reveal the "Peace Rock"--a divine sign which it is the duty of Hathi to interpret--he declares the "Water Truce" (p. 80). As the narrator comments, the truce ensures continuance of life in a time dominated by the enemy common to all animals--death. Thus, according to the truce, "it is death to kill at the drinking place when once the Water Truce has been declared. The reason of this is that drinking comes before eating" (p. 80). So it is that "the Jungle people came up, starved and weary, to the shrunken river,--tiger, bear, deer, buffalo, and pig, all together,--drank the fouled waters" (p. 81). The Law reduces all distinctions in times of crisis, all the animals being forced into an altruistic concern for one another.

The necessity for a Law in the Jungle, however, is a direct result of the "Fall" from grace. As Hathi--in this case the story-teller within the story--reveals, before the fall there was no law that confined the animals, but the Law of Harmony. "Before the Jungle People knew of Man" (p. 91) they lived together, states Hathi, "making one people" in a land of plenty, where "there was no drought, and leaves and flowers and fruit grew on the same tree" (p. 91). But, one fateful day, the "First of the Tigers" arbiter of the Jungle, while watching a dispute between two bucks, "forgot that he was the Master and the Judge of the Jungle" (p. 92) and killed one of the Bucks. Thus, anarchy displaced the natural harmony. To put an end to the chaos, Tha created a "Law that ye must not break. Now ye shall know Fear, and when ye have found him ye shall know that he is your master and the rest shall follow" (p. 94), and so it is, concludes Hathi, that the law of Fear separates the "tribes," like "keeping to like" (p. 95). However, the memory of life before the Fall continues in the collective unconscious of the Jungle People and "when there is one great Fear over all, as there is now," states Hathi, "can we of the Jungle lay aside our little fears and meet together in one place as we do now" (p. 100).

The Law of the Jungle thus ensures the continuity of life, and individuality is kept subordinate to this basic desire for ongoingness. This is the lesson Mowgli has to learn. While the "strength of the Pack is the Wolf," as the Law of the Wolves states, the "strength of the Wolf is the Pack." Mowgli is so full of his own importance, of being "Master of the Jungle," that he forgets the latter half of the Law. In "The Spring Running," he is forced to face the fact the Jungle will continue to exist, irrespective of whether he does so or not. It is only during the first few days of Spring that Mowgli loses his power over the Jungle People, who forget all laws except that of Spring. At such a time, Mowgli's call to his brothers goes unanswered, for they are "far beyond earshot, singing over the spring songs . . . with the wolves of the Pack" (p. 269). Anger at his inability to dictate to the Jungle People makes him pose what he believes to be a rhetorical question: "Am I master of the Jungle or am I not ?" (p. 271) He has to find the correct answer which is negative rather than affirmative. From the moment that he poses the question, Mowgli begins his journey away from the Jungle. He is, in fact, in the process of discovering that not only is he not Master of the Jungle, but the Jungle Laws are no longer meaningful to him--a frightening discovery to make. The advent of Spring evokes a particular type of response from the Jungle People, who pay homage to the deity by indulging in sexual activity, thus ensuring new life in the Jungle, as Spring ensures new life in Nature. Mowgli is a witness to this form of self-expression and he hears "them grunting and screaming and whistling according to their kind" (p. 267). He is, irrevocably an outsider to such expression and his growth from innocence to experience entails the painful recognition that it is so. Though he may be the "strength" of his "Pack," it is only the "Pack" of Man that can be his strength.

To Mowgli, however, his self seems to be a chaotic mass of contradictory impulses. The Jungle, his beloved home, no longer satisfies him. Not accustomed to cerebral introspection, Mowgli--who thinks through his stomach--believes he has eaten "poison," but it is merely the same poison that the children of the zodiac ate, and The Boy touched in the form of cold iron. It is the burden of "self-fulfilment" that is on Mowgli,[26] and this, as Gilbert rightly points out, is the "Law." It is this law that turns Mowgli from the Jungle as Kaa in his wisdom knows: "Man goes to Man at the last, though the Jungle does not cast him out" (p. 290). Like The Boy in "Cold Iron," he snaps the ring around his neck himself. The Boy, after locking the "new, heavy, shining slave ring" (p. 22), questions: "What else could have I done ?" (p. 23) and similarly, there is nothing Mowgli can do to prevent his growth into manhood. "That Spring," as he tells Bagheera, "his stomach was changed in him" (p.267). Everything that pleased him before, is meaningless to him in his new condition. Even the "spring running"--this time undertaken in the hope of outrunning his inexplicable condition--leaves him struck with an "unhappiness . . . ten times worse than before" (p. 274). The only logical explanation which suggests itself to Mowgli is death, and the belief that he is approaching the end, and in reality it is the death of him as he knows himself. But, he seems to know that death is not going to be physical. Akela's dying words predicting this approaching death reverberate in his mind. "Thou art a man" he had said. "Go to thine own people."[27] His reply at the time comes unbidden to memory. "When Mowgli drives out Mowgli, I will go" (p. 255) he had said, and now that the time which he believed would never come, has come, he refuses to accept the death. "I *am* of the Jungle" (p. 276) he argues in desperation, and without conviction, knowing full well that he is not part of the Jungle any more, and the burden of the consciousness of this fact is on him. To stay would be to be false to himself, go he must. It is significant that psychologically at war with himself, Mowgli goes to the Man Pack for relief, more specifically, to Messua. It is facing her that he achieves his moment of realization. "I am Nathoo" he says, when she asks him "art thou him I called Nathoo ?" (p. 281) and for the first time, Mowgli/

Nathoo learns the law of the Family and "all manners of strange feelings that he had never felt before were running over him" (p. 282). Return to the Jungle is not possible. When Mowgli makes an attempt to go back, "Mother I go" (p. 285), he is aware that he must return: "I will surely come back" (p. 285). The sight of a "girl" helps seal his fate. As Kaa states in one of his many moments of wisdom, "Having cast the skin, we may not creep into it afresh. It is the Law" (p. 291).

Back in the Jungle, Mowgli is forced to admit that it is not "any poison" which has caused the change in him, but his own self that demands its release from the laws of the Jungle in order to discover and create laws of its own. He expresses this in metaphors: "I run the Spring running, but I am not made still. I bathe but I am not made a cool. . . The Red Flower is in my body, my bones are water--and--I know not what I know" (p. 290). All Mowgli is certain of is the necessity of moving out of the Jungle, heartbreaking as the break will be. "I would not go," he sobs, "but I am drawn by both feet" (p. 291). Thus, Mowgli follows the dictates of his own consciousness in order to create his own laws. But he does not go alone to a "new hunting trail"; he has been initiated into the mysteries of existence by Baloo and carries this knowledge with him into the world of experience, of men. The years of learning under the wise guidance of Baloo provide the foundation for his new life. It is with the assurance that he has a knowledge of the Law that Mowgli leaves the land of innocence to find self-fulfilment in the land of the unknown. With him goes the blessing of the Jungle:

> In the dawns when thou shalt wake
> To the toil thou canst not break,
> Heartsick for the Jungle's sake:
> Wood and Water, Wind and Tree,
> Wisdom, Strength, and Courtesy,
> Jungle-Favour go with thee !
> (p. 295)

V

Though part of Kipling's vision is a realistic analysis of the chaos which finds expression in alienation, psychological disintegration, and fearful death therefore, he is at the same time inspired by his "daemon" to hold up to Man a vision of Paradise that probably exists on earth, except that--as Gobind believes--"we have not the faith to see."[28] It is in this belief in the power of love, the imagination and the Law which dictates self-fulfilment, that Kipling seems to have found the essentials necessary to make his vision the "faith" common to all mankind. Tales that plumb the dark night of man's soul and tales that offer redemption from contraries of the same impulse of the Imagination which creates them in order to reveal the vision of a unity in existence that is divine.

It is only for the sake of discussion that the abstract qualities of love, imagination, law and death, alienation, and psychological disintegration have been separated. There exists a unity between them which makes them indivisible. In an after-dinner speech that he gave to the Royal Society of Medicine titled "Healing by the Stars," Kipling argued that "the essential unity of creation" is echoed in man, who "is himself a universe of universes, each universe ordered--negatively and positively--by sympathy and antipathy--on the same lines as hold the stars in their courses."[29] This is the vision that the "Crystal-eyed Sages of Ionia" vouchsafe to fallen man, who ultimately turns from the "shadows and the shows" of the Blakian followers of Nobodaddy, "anxious priests and wizards," to discover the truth:

> . . . one Breath in all things,
> That blows all things between
> They proved one Matter in all things--
> Eternal, changeless, unseen,
> 'That the heart of the Matter was single
> Till the Breath should bid it bring forth--
> Even as men whispered in Ionia. . . .
> All things known upon earth.[30]

NOTES

1. Rudyard Kipling, "La Nuit Blanche," *Rudyard Kipling's Verse* (New York: Doubleday, Doran and Co., 1928), p. 29. All references to

Kipling's poems, unless otherwise stated, are to this collection.

2. D.M.E. Roskies, "Telling the Truth in Kipling and Freud," *English*, xxxi, Spring 1982, p. 17.

3. Ibid., p. 17.

4. Juan Mascaro, in the introduction to *The Upanishads* (Harmondsworth: Penguin, 1965), states that the "Holy Spirit may be the nearest translation of Brahman in Christian language," and Brahma is the "manifestation of Brahman as creator" (p.11).

5. Rudyard Kipling, "A Recantation," *Rudyard Kipling's Verse*, p. 424.

6. The Bible, *John*, I:i.

7. John Milton, *Paradise Lost* in *John Milton: Complete Poems and Major Prose*, ed. Merritt Y. Hughes (Indianapolis: The Odyssey Press, 1957). In Book III, Milton announces that he finds recompense for his blindness in the access to "celestial light" which shines "inward" and allows him to "see and tell / Of things invisible to mortal sight." Refer to lines 51-55.

8. In *Something of Myself* (VIII), Kipling states that "My Daemon was with me in the *Jungle Books*, *Kim* and both Puck books." Quoted by Dobree in *Rudyard Kipling: Realist and Fabulist* (London: Oxford U. Press, 1967), p. 12.

9. Rudyard Kipling, "The Children of the Zodiac," *Many Inventions* (New York: D. Appleton and Co., 1894), p. 400. The tale was first published in the *Harper's Weekly*, Dec. 5. All references to this tale are to this edition.

10. Rudyard Kipling, "Naboth," *Life's Handicap, Being Stories of Mine Own People* (New York: Macmillan, 1896), p. 71.

11. Preface to *Life's Handicap*, p. xi.

12. Ibid., p. xii.

13. "L'envoi."

14. Rudyard Kipling, *Kim* (New York: Charles Scribner, 1903), p. 18. All references to the text are to this edition.

15. Elliot L. Gilbert, *The Good Kipling* (Oberlin: Ohio U. Press, 1970), p. 163.

16. "L'envoi."

17. The term is taken from Van Gennep's book titled *Rites of Passage* (Chicago: U. of Chicago Press, 1960). It is used by Gennep to refer to the periods of transition in every individual's life, when he

moved from one state of being to the next, the major periods being that of birth, puberty, marriage and death.

18. Rudyard Kipling, "The Finances of the Gods," *Life's Handicap*, p. 23.

19. C. A. Bodelsen, *Aspects of Kipling's Art* (Manchester: Manchester U. Press, 1964), p. 49.

20. Rudyard Kipling, *Kim*, p. 472.

21. Noel Annan, "Kipling's Place in the History of Ideas," *Kipling's Mind and Art*, ed. Andrew Rutherford (Edinburgh: Oliver and Boyd, 1965), p. 119.

22. Elliot L. Gilbert, *The Good Kipling*, p. 185.

23. In "La Nuit Blanche," the poet describes his feelings of responsibility concerning the evil he sees around him and his desire to rectify it. I quote a representative stanza:

> Half the night I watched the Heavens
> Fizz like '81 champagne--
> Fly to sixes and to sevens
> Wheel and thunder back again:
> And when all was peace and order
> Save one planet nailed askew
> Much I wept because my warder
> Would not let me set it true.
>
> (p. 30)

24. Angus Wilson, *The Strange Ride of Rudyard Kipling* (London: Granada Publishing Ltd., 1979), p. 172.

25. Rudyard Kipling, "How Fear Came," *Jungle Book* in *The Works of Rudyard Kipling* (New York: Charles Scribner's Sons, 1897), Vol. 7, p. 77. All references to the tale and *Jungle Book* are to this edition.

26. Elliot L. Gilbert in *The Good Kipling* states that "for Kipling . . . the 'Law' of the universe manifests itself most clearly and fully in the order and necessity of each man's nature. In the last of the *Jungle Book* stories, 'The Spring Running' for instance, the primary Law of the Jungle is very specifically identified with this 'burden of self-accomplishment' with the obligation of every organism to discover and fulfil itself" (pp. 46-47).

27. Rudyard Kipling, "Red Dog," *Jungle Book*, p. 255.

28. Rudyard Kipling, "The Finances of the Gods," *Life's Handicap*, p. 23.

29. Quoted by Dobrée, p. 26.

30. The companion poem to "Unprofessional," a tale in *Limits and Renewals* (London: Macmillan, 1932). The poem is titled "The Threshold" and is on p. 284.

APPENDIX

A List of Kipling's Short Stories

Title	*Year of Publication*
"At the End of the Passage"	1890
"Beyond the Pale"	1888
"Bisara of Pooree"	1888
"Bubbling Well Road"	1888
"By Word of Mouth"	1887
"Children of the Zodiac, The"	1891
"City of Dreadful Night, The"	1890
"Cold Iron"	1909
"Dream of Duncan Parrenness, The"	1889
"False Dawn"	1888
"Finances of the Gods, The"	1887
"Gate of the Hundred Sorrows, The"	1884
"How Fear Came"	1892
"Man Who Would Be King, The"	1889
"Mark of the Beast, The"	1890
"Phantom Richshaw, The"	1888
"Strange Ride of Morrowbie Jukes, The"	1885
"Thrown Away"	1888
"To be Filed for Reference"	1888
"Wandering Jew, The"	1888
"Without Benefit of Clergy"	1890
"Wressley of the Foreign Office"	1887